Cambridge Elements

Elements in Phonology
edited by
Robert Kennedy
University of California, Santa Barbara
Patrycja Strycharczuk
University of Manchester

ISSUES IN METRICAL PHONOLOGY

Insights from Ukrainian

Beata Łukaszewicz
University of Warsaw

Janina Mołczanow
University of Warsaw

CAMBRIDGE
UNIVERSITY PRESS

Shaftesbury Road, Cambridge CB2 8EA, United Kingdom

One Liberty Plaza, 20th Floor, New York, NY 10006, USA

477 Williamstown Road, Port Melbourne, VIC 3207, Australia

314–321, 3rd Floor, Plot 3, Splendor Forum, Jasola District Centre, New Delhi – 110025, India

103 Penang Road, #05–06/07, Visioncrest Commercial, Singapore 238467

Cambridge University Press is part of Cambridge University Press & Assessment, a department of the University of Cambridge.

We share the University's mission to contribute to society through the pursuit of education, learning and research at the highest international levels of excellence.

www.cambridge.org
Information on this title: www.cambridge.org/9781009517454

DOI: 10.1017/9781009447164

© Beata Łukaszewicz and Janina Mołczanow 2025

This publication is in copyright. Subject to statutory exception and to the provisions of relevant collective licensing agreements, with the exception of the Creative Commons version the link for which is provided below, no reproduction of any part may take place without the written permission of Cambridge University Press & Assessment.

An online version of this work is published at doi.org/10.1017/9781009447164 under a Creative Commons Open Access license CC-BY-NC 4.0 which permits re-use, distribution and reproduction in any medium for non-commercial purposes providing appropriate credit to the original work is given and any changes made are indicated. To view a copy of this license visit https://creativecommons.org/licenses/by-nc/4.0

When citing this work, please include a reference to the DOI 10.1017/9781009447164

First published 2025

A catalogue record for this publication is available from the British Library

ISBN 978-1-009-51745-4 Hardback
ISBN 978-1-009-44714-0 Paperback
ISSN 2633-9064 (online)
ISSN 2633-9056 (print)

Cambridge University Press & Assessment has no responsibility for the persistence or accuracy of URLs for external or third-party internet websites referred to in this publication and does not guarantee that any content on such websites is, or will remain, accurate or appropriate.

Issues in Metrical Phonology

Insights from Ukrainian

Elements in Phonology

DOI: 10.1017/9781009447164
First published online: February 2025

Beata Łukaszewicz
University of Warsaw

Janina Mołczanow
University of Warsaw

Author for correspondence: Beata Łukaszewicz, b.lukaszewicz@uw.edu.pl

Abstract: Metrical systems differ in patterns of stress assignment, the domains over which those patterns are built, and acoustic manifestations of stress. It has been widely debated in the phonological/phonetic literature how stress should be represented, what mechanisms govern its assignment, and whether the phonetic underpinnings of primary/secondary stress exist independently of other prominence effects (e.g. boundary strengthening, pitch accents). This Element addresses these fundamental issues on the basis of an in-depth study of a hybrid (lexical-grammatical) metrical system of Ukrainian. It synthesises previous results with new findings, focusing on the phonetic as well as formal description of the Ukrainian system. The lexical-grammatical stress interactions in Ukrainian pose a challenge for current metrical theories and shed light both on the relation between the lexical and grammatical stress domains and on the relationship between categorical and gradient aspects of the metrical system. This title is also available as Open Access on Cambridge Core.

Keywords: lexical stress, grammatical stress, metrical phonology, phonetics, Ukrainian

© Beata Łukaszewicz and Janina Mołczanow 2025

ISBNs: 9781009517454 (HB), 9781009447140 (PB), 9781009447164 (OC)
ISSNs: 2633-9064 (online), 2633-9056 (print)

Contents

1 Introduction   1

2 Case Study: The Hybrid (Lexical-Grammatical) Stress System of Ukrainian   5

3 Discussion and Directions for Future Research   46

    References   58

1 Introduction

An important aspect of linguistic organisation is metrical structure, which assigns relative prominences to syllables within a prosodic domain. Metrical systems differ in patterns of stress assignment, the domains over which these patterns are built, and acoustic manifestations of stress. In this section, we discuss the cross-linguistic diversity of stress systems and the major challenges it poses for the metrical theory. We focus here on word-level stress, setting up the background for the case study of a hybrid lexical-grammatical stress system, Ukrainian, presented in detail in Section 2. The complexity of the Ukrainian system allows us to address those major challenges, shedding light on some general mechanisms underlying metrical systems. In Section 3, we suggest a model of mutual interaction between lexical and rhythmic stress, in which rhythmic stress is assigned with reference to the lexically specified location of primary stress, and the domain of phonetic manifestation of lexical stress is further delimited by the position of rhythmic beats, specified by the phonological grammar.

1.1 Lexical versus Grammatical Stress Systems

In some languages, word stress is specified lexically; in others, it is predicted by the grammar. Lexical stress systems, despite having unpredictable stress, may also exhibit grammatical conditioning ('default stress'), or be influenced by other factors (lexical frequencies, segmental distribution) in circumstances where lexical specifications of stress are unavailable (see e.g. Revithiadou & Lengeris 2016 on the default stress in Greek; Mołczanow *et al.* 2019a on the default stress in Russian). Grammatical stress systems – that is, systems having predictable stress – are not devoid of lexically specified exceptions, a well-known case being Polish, which has a predominantly regular penultimate stress pattern and a handful of lexical exceptions with antepenultimate stress (e.g. *gra'matyk+a* 'grammar', *uni'wersytet* 'university'), usually analysed in terms of extrametricality (i.e. marking of the final syllable as invisible to stress rules; Franks 1985; Rubach & Booij 1985; Halle & Vergnaud 1987; Łukaszewicz & Mołczanow *to appear*). Nevertheless, lexical and grammatical stress systems pose different descriptive and theoretical challenges, which is reflected in analytical tools – to a large extent developed separately for those two types of systems. The intricacies of the Ukrainian metrical system, which has a complex interaction between lexical and grammatical stress, will be analysed to improve our understanding of the mechanisms underlying stress assignment and the interaction between lexical and grammatical stress domains. Following the earlier work (Łukaszewicz & Mołczanow 2018a,

2018b; Mołczanow & Łukaszewicz 2021), a unified integrative approach to lexical and grammatical stress will be adopted.

1.2 Metrical Systems with Two Levels of Stress

Some metrical systems have both primary and secondary stress; as a consequence, cross-linguistically diverse patterns of interaction between primary and secondary levels of prominence occur. Secondary stress may depend on the word's morphological structure – that is, it may result from preserving the primary stress of stems as a secondary stress in derived forms; consider the English pair *imagine* [ɪˈmædʒɪn] – *imagination* [ɪˌmædʒɪˈneɪʃᵊn] (e.g. Chomsky & Halle 1968; Prince 1983; Pater 2000). It may also be purely rhythmic, based exclusively on metrical principles and thus independent of morphology; compare the Polish quadruplet: *pomidor* [pɔˈmidɔr] 'tomato (N. nom. sg.)' – *pomidora* [ˌpɔmiˈdɔr+a] (N. gen. sg.) – *pomidorowy* [ˌpɔmidɔˈr+ɔv+ɨ] 'tomato (Adj. nom. sg.)' – *pomidorowego* [ˌpɔmiˌdɔr+ɔˈv+ɛgɔ] (Adj. gen. sg.), where rhythmic stresses appear on odd-numbered syllables as long as no clash with primary stress ensues (Rubach & Booij 1985; Kraska-Szlenk 2003; Łukaszewicz 2015, 2018). Here we focus on the latter types of systems. Two mechanisms of the purely rhythmic stress assignment are relevant from the point of view of the Ukrainian system analysed in Section 2. First, rhythmic stress can appear at edges, as in 'hammock' (Elenbaas & Kager 1999: 309), 'dual' (Gordon 2002: 495ff), or 'polar' systems (van der Hulst 1996 *et seq.*). Second, it can be iterative, resulting in cross-linguistic differences in the directionality of rhythmic stress assignment. We illustrate the directionality effects in (1) on the basis of grammatical metrical systems such as Polish (Rubach & Booij 1985; Kraska-Szlenk 2003; Łukaszewicz 2015, 2018, Łukaszewicz *et al.* 2018), Garawa (Furby 1974) and Warao (Osborn 1966, after Kager 2001: 15).

(1) *Directionality of rhythmic stress assignment*
    a. [(ˌσσ) (ˌσσ) σ (ˈσσ)] (e.g. Polish)   *bidirectional*
    b. [(ˈσσ) σ (ˌσσ) (ˌσσ)] (e.g. Garawa)   *bidirectional*
    c. [σ (ˌσσ) (ˌσσ) (ˈσσ)] (e.g. Warao)   *unidirectional*

In those systems, (feet containing) rhythmic beats 'ripple away' either from the edges (the left edge in (1a), the right edge in (1b)) or from primary stress (as in (1c)), resulting in two different directionality patterns. In (1a) and (1b), which are bidirectional stress systems, lapses (i.e. sequences of two unstressed syllables) are located near the peak (primary stress); in (1c), which is a unidirectional system, there is no lapse.

Bidirectionality effects can be obtained through competing theoretical mechanisms: rhythmic constraints (Lapse-at-Peak, 'lapses are located near the peak'; Kager 2001) versus gradient alignment, pushing rhythmic stresses towards the left or right edge of the word.[1] The latter can be formulated in relation to intermediate prosodic structure constituents, feet (Align-Ft-L/R, 'the left/right edge of every foot is aligned with the left/right edge of a prosodic word'; McCarthy & Prince 1993) or in relation to prominence marks on the metrical grid (Gordon 2002; Mołczanow & Łukaszewicz 2021). This raises additional questions concerning stress representation (Hermans 2011; Mołczanow & Łukaszewicz 2021). (For extensive typological analyses of the world's grammatical stress systems in terms of grid- or foot-based representations, see e.g. Gordon 2002 and Martínez-Paricio & Kager 2015, respectively). The Ukrainian system has purely grammatical rhythmic stress, whose propagation resembles the bidirectional systems in (1a–b). However, it is more complex as it exhibits simultaneously the rightward and leftward rhythmic stress iteration from the word's edges towards the lexical stress position, which can be any syllable in the word. As we will demonstrate in Section 2, lapses can occur simultaneously to the left and to the right of the peak. Elaborating on the initial proposal in Mołczanow and Łukaszewicz (2021), we argue that the Ukrainian metrical system poses a challenge for the mechanism of gradient alignment and calls for restoring rhythmic constraints as a universal mechanism governing directionality effects. It also requires that grid representations be assumed. In Section 3, we suggest a model of the interaction between lexical and rhythmic stress, in which the location of primary stress is specified lexically, but the domain of its phonetic manifestation is defined depending on the position of rhythmic beats represented in terms of grids and determined by high-ranked Lapse-at-Peak.

1.3 Phonetic Grounding of Stress and Its Interaction with Other Phenomena

Languages also differ in how metrical prominence is expressed phonetically, and how stress interacts with other types of prominence, such as prosodic boundary strengthening or phrasal pitch accents (see discussions in Beckman 1986; Hayes 1995; Ladd 1996). Acoustic evidence for secondary stress has notoriously proved weaker relative to primary stress (e.g. Garellek & White 2015; Gordon & Roettger 2017; Łukaszewicz 2018). Gordon and Roettger (2017: 7) provide numerous examples of studies in which 'vowels claimed in

---

[1] Rhythmic constraints, such as Lapse-at-Peak, as well as the mechanism of gradient alignment have received a substantial degree of criticism; see Buckley (2009) for a summary of the relevant literature. The main problematic aspects of those mechanisms mentioned in the literature are their non-local character and/or making reference to non-constituent structures (such as 'lapses').

the phonological literature to carry secondary stress were not different from unstressed vowels along any dimension'. Apart from being optional, rhythmic stress may not be cued by vowel parameters, which has critically hindered its detection in some phonetic studies; for example, see Łukaszewicz (2015, 2018) on the consonantal rhythm in Polish, which is associated with lengthening of consonants in the onset of a stressed syllable. Stress may also interact with segmental phenomena in various ways, shedding light on the relationship between the categorical and gradient levels of linguistic description. The presence of different degrees of vowel reduction in Russian, which is non-categorical in the second pretonic position (i.e. position separated by one syllable to the left from the lexical stress), but categorical in the first pretonic position (i.e. position immediately preceding lexical stress), mediated by the presence of lengthening in that position (Barnes 2006), may serve as an example.

As we will demonstrate in Section 2, Ukrainian shows an interesting interplay between categorical and gradient aspects of the prosodic system. The edge-based rhythmic stress is found to be independent of boundary strengthening effects and phrasal accents. Apart from lexical and rhythmic stresses being cued by enhanced duration, there is an additional effect involving the temporal dimension in Ukrainian – pretonic lengthening, which we view as a lexical stress domain extension in the phonetic domain. In the phonological domain, the extent of this effect seems to depend on the position of rhythmic beats, as determined by Lapse-at-Peak. In the phonetic domain, the presence of this effect hinders the duration-based expression of rhythmic stress in the vicinity of lexical stress. It also creates an asymmetry in the temporal patterns across the syllables to the left and to the right of the lexical stress. We also look at the potential effect of duration on formant undershoot depending on stress and position within the word. The Ukrainian data shed light on the relationship between lexical and grammatical stress domains not only in terms of formal organisation but also physical parameters.

1.4 Goals of the Current Study

In this Element, we discuss various aspects of metrical organisation and its surface manifestations vis-à-vis competing theoretical constructs. We focus on issues which have continued to be central in the phonological/phonetic debate since the seminal work of Liberman and Prince (1977), Hayes (1980, 1995), Prince (1983, 1990), and Halle and Vergnaud (1987):

(i) How is stress represented phonologically (in terms of metrical grids or metrical feet)?

(ii) What mechanisms govern directionality of stress assignment? Specifically, do rhythmic constraints such as LAPSE-AT-PEAK play a role, despite some arguments against those constraints raised in the past? Relatedly, what is the relationship between the domain of primary stress and that of secondary stress?
(iii) What are the phonetic underpinnings of primary/secondary stress? Are they independent of other prosodic effects (e.g. boundary strengthening effects) possibly coded by the same phonetic parameters?

All those central questions will be addressed on the basis of our in-depth case study of the hybrid metrical system of Ukrainian, presented in Section 2. Characteristics of the Ukrainian system make it an excellent testing ground for competing theoretical mechanisms proposed in the metrical literature. The theoretical considerations are supported empirically by acoustic data pertaining to the Ukrainian stress patterns.

2 Case Study: The Hybrid (Lexical-Grammatical) Stress System of Ukrainian

2.1 Introduction

This section provides a systematic exploration of the metrical system of Ukrainian. We begin the discussion by laying out basic generalisations concerning the Ukrainian stress system (Section 2.1.1), based on traditional grammars of Ukrainian, such as Bilodid (1969), Žovtobrjux (1973), Hryščenko (2002), and Plušč (2009), among others. According to these standard sources as well as more recent acoustic studies (Łukaszewicz & Mołczanow 2018a, 2018b), Ukrainian combines lexical and grammatical stress. Primary (lexical) stress is weight-insensitive and can occur in any syllable in a word; secondary stress is predictably placed at the word's edges and on every other syllable, forming alternating rhythmic patterns with lapses near lexical stress.

Next, we present the phonological analysis of the metrical system of Ukrainian (Section 2.1.2). We argue that foot-based and grid-based approaches developed within contemporary metrical theory are unable to capture the stress directionality and the placement of lapses resulting from the interaction between lexical and grammatical stresses in Ukrainian. We address these challenges by adopting a hybrid theoretical framework that combines grid-based representations with the licencing constraint LAPSE-AT-PEAK. The theoretical discussion sets the stage for the acoustic studies of the Ukrainian metrical system, inspired by the predictions of the phonological model introduced in Section 2.1.2.

The remainder of this section reports on the experimental research addressing the intricacies of the Ukrainian prosodic system. We review the findings of our previous acoustic studies (Section 2.2), and present the results of a new experiment (Section 2.3). Overall, these results align with the traditional (often impressionistic) descriptions of the Ukrainian stress, postulating the existence of alternating secondary stresses. As we will see, two additional facts about the prosodic system of Ukrainian are revealed by the recent research. First, the experiments consistently show that syllables immediately preceding the lexically stressed syllable (pretonic syllables) tend to have a longer duration than might be expected based on their metrically weak position. In contrast, no similar lengthening is observed across the syllables immediately following the stressed syllable (posttonic syllables), meaning there is no acoustic symmetry in the syllables immediately preceding and following lexical stress. Second, there is no acoustic symmetry concerning secondary stresses to the left and to the right of lexical stress. With respect to the former, acoustic measurements point to duration as a consistent cue to initial and medial secondary stress in longer words (in which lexical stress is separated from the left word edge by at least four syllables, e.g. [ˌunʲiˌʋersɨˈtɛt] 'university, nom. sg.'), whereas the initial syllable in shorter words (such as [ˌmafiaˈzɨn] 'shop, nom. sg.' and [ˌpɛrɛkɔˈnaʋ] 'persuade, past. masc.') is not significantly longer than the following unstressed syllable. No such difference is observed to the right of lexical stress, where secondary stresses are uniformly expressed by duration. These asymmetries are formally modelled in Section 3, in which we suggest that, in addition to lexically stressed syllable, the domain of lexical stress in Ukrainian should be extended leftwards to comprise up to three pretonic syllables, depending on the assignment of rhythmic beats.

The discussion of the acoustic correlates of Ukrainian stress is based on the corpus of data which we have accumulated over the past several years. The corpus contains around ten hours of recorded speech. The data, collected in sixty-five sessions from forty-five participants, comprises words (citation forms) placed in frames. Test items are of different length (two to eight syllables) and are stressed on different syllables. In this Element, new data from the corpus will be analysed and the findings will be synthesised with our previous acoustic studies.

2.1.1 Descriptive Generalisations

Ukrainian has an interesting prosodic system because it combines free lexical stress with predictable grammatical stress, which enter into a complex interaction. Lexical stress in Ukrainian is weight-insensitive and there is no

Table 1 Stress patterns in nominal stems

	Fixed stress		**Mobile stress**	
Nom. Sg.	rɔˈdɪn+a	ʒittʲ+ˈa	t͡ʃɔlɔˈvʲik	nɔʋɪn+ˈa
Gen. Sg.	rɔˈdɪn+ɪ	ʒittʲ+ˈa	t͡ʃɔlɔˈvʲik+a	nɔʋɪn+ˈɪ
Dat. Sg.	rɔˈdɪnʲ+i	ʒittʲ+ˈu	t͡ʃɔlɔˈvʲik+ɔvʲi	nɔʋɪnʲ+ˈi
Acc. Sg.	rɔˈdɪn+u	ʒittʲ+ˈa	t͡ʃɔlɔˈvʲik+a	nɔʋɪn+ˈu
Instr. Sg.	rɔˈdɪn+ɔju	ʒittʲ+ˈam	t͡ʃɔlɔˈvʲik+ɔm	nɔʋɪn+ˈɔju
Loc. Sg.	rɔˈdɪnʲ+i	ʒittʲ+ˈi	t͡ʃɔlɔˈvʲik+u	nɔʋɪnʲ+ˈi
Voc. Sg.	rɔˈdɪn+ɔ	ʒittʲ+ˈa	t͡ʃɔlɔˈvʲit͡ʃ+ɛ	nɔˈʋɪn+ɔ
Nom. Pl.	rɔˈdɪn+ɪ	ʒittʲ+ˈa	t͡ʃɔlɔvʲik+ˈɪ	nɔˈʋɪn+ɪ
Gen. Pl.	rɔˈdɪn	ʒittʲ+ˈiʋ	t͡ʃɔlɔvʲikʲ+ˈiʋ	nɔˈʋɪn
Dat. Pl.	rɔˈdɪn+am	ʒittʲ+ˈam	t͡ʃɔlɔvʲik+ˈam	nɔˈʋɪn+am
Acc. Pl.	rɔˈdɪn+ɪ	ʒittʲ+ˈa	t͡ʃɔlɔvʲikʲ+ˈiʋ	nɔˈʋɪn+ɪ
Instr. Pl.	rɔˈdɪn+amɪ	ʒittʲ+ˈamɪ	t͡ʃɔlɔvʲik+ˈamɪ	nɔˈʋɪn+amɪ
Loc. Sg.	rɔˈdɪn+ax	ʒittʲ+ˈax	t͡ʃɔlɔvʲik+ˈax	nɔˈʋɪn+ax
Voc. Sg.	rɔˈdɪn+ɪ	ʒittʲ+ˈa	t͡ʃɔlɔvʲik+ˈɪ	nɔˈʋɪn+ɪ
	'family'	'life'	'man'	'news'

phonemic length. Ukrainian has a six-vowel system /i, ɪ,[2] u, ɛ, ɔ, a/ (Toc'ka 1969). Primary (lexical) stress can appear on any syllable in a word, for example, [ˈdɔrɔɦɔ] 'dear, adv.' [dɔˈrɔɦa] 'way, nom. sg.', [dɔrɔˈɦa] 'dear, nom. sg. fem'. Although the location of stress is largely unpredictable, there exist several morphologically conditioned accentual paradigms in Ukrainian. Similarly to the other East Slavic languages (Russian and Belarusian), stress in Ukrainian can be either fixed on one syllable or alternate between different syllables within inflectional paradigms (Stankiewicz 1993), as illustrated by the stress patterns in the nominal stems in Table 1.

Let us observe that stress can be fixed on the stem, as in [rɔˈdɪn+a] 'family', on the ending, as in [ʒittʲ+ˈa] 'life', or alternate between the stem and the ending in mobile stress patterns. In [t͡ʃɔlɔˈvʲik] 'man', for instance, the final syllable of

---

[2] We use the IPA symbol [ɪ] to transcribe a vowel which is spelled 'и' in the Ukrainian orthography and which is described as high and front in the phonetic literature; compare Toc'ka (1973: 109). Let us note that this vowel is transcribed as [ɪ] by Pompino-Marschall *et al.* (2017), who justify their choice of this symbol by the fact that the Ukrainian vowel differs phonetically from the Russian [ɨ]. However, the use of the symbol [ɪ] for Ukrainian is contestable on both phonetic and phonological grounds. Phonologically, this vowel patterns together with back vowels in Ukrainian (Łukaszewicz *et al.* submitted). In addition, Vakulenko (2018: 205–206) adduces several pieces of phonetically based evidence supporting the use of the symbol [ɪ] for Ukrainian. Following Steriopolo (2012: 55), he concludes that 'the Ukrainian /и/ is a front retracted vowel close to [ɪ]' (Vakulenko 2018: 205).

the stem is stressed throughout the inflectional paradigm in the singular, whereas the inflectional ending is stressed in the plural. The opposite pattern is observed in [nɔʋin+ˈa] 'news', in which stress is located on the stem in the plural and, with the exception of the voc. sg. form [nɔˈʋin+ɔ], on the ending in the singular. Let us also note that, as in any system with lexical stress, there exist lexical items which exhibit variation in the location of the primary (lexical) stress, for example, [ˈpɔmɨlka] ~ [pɔˈmɨlka] 'mistake, nom. sg.', [ˈtakɔʒ] ~ [taˈkɔʒ] 'also', [ʋɛsˈnʲanij] ~ [ʋɛsnʲaˈnij] 'spring, adj. nom. sg.'.

In addition, both descriptive grammars and recent acoustic research point to the existence of secondary (rhythmic) stress in Ukrainian, which is assigned at the word's edges, as well as on every other syllable, forming a predictable alternating pattern with lapses near lexical stress (Nakonečnyj 1969; Toc'ka 2002; Łukaszewicz & Mołczanow 2018a, 2018b). Let us point out that modern Ukrainian displays considerable dialectal diversity (Shevelov 1979), which is particularly evident in the differences in the patterns of lexical stress placement. Yet, there is agreement in the literature that secondary stress is present both in the standard literary language (Nakonečnyj 1969), which is based on the south-eastern dialectal group, and in the standard Ukrainian spoken in the west of the country (Łukaszewicz & Mołczanow 2018a, 2018b, 2018c).³

Data in (2) illustrate possible rhythmic patterns for words consisting of three to seven syllables (longer words are rare in Ukrainian).

(2)   *Rhythmic patterns in words of different length*
    a. *Three-syllable words*
       ˈσσˌσ   [ˈrʲiʃɛˌnnʲa] 'decision, nom. sg.'
       σˈσσ   [t͡ʃaˈstɨna] 'part, nom. sg.'
       ˌσσˈσ   [ˌmafiaˈzɨn] 'shop, nom. sg.'⁴

    b. *Four-syllable words*
       ˈσσσˌσ   [ˈsprɔbuʋaˌti] 'try, inf.'
       σˈσσˌσ   [ʋaˈrɛnɨˌki] 'dumpling, nom. pl.'
       ˌσσˈσσ   [ˌkɔrɔˈlɛʋa] 'queen, nom. sg.'
       ˌσσσˈσ   [ˌpɛrɛkɔˈnaʋ] 'persuade, past. masc.'

    c. *Five-syllable words*
       ˈσσˌσσˌσ   [ˈʋɨkɔˌrɨstaˌnnʲa] 'use, nom. sg.
       σˈσσσˌσ   [kɔmˈpanʲijɛˌju] 'company, instr. sg.'

---

³ One exception is Brovčenko (1969: 16), who in her book-length study of word stress of Ukrainian notes briefly that secondary stress is only present in compounds in this language.

⁴ Our previous acoustic research as well as the results of the experiment reported in the present study have not found reliable acoustic cues to word-initial secondary stress in [ˌσσˈσ(σ)] and [ˌσσσˈσ(σ)]. Nevertheless, we transcribe this stress here and in the remainder of this Element because, as is indicated in Section 2.4 and further argued in Section 3, this stress is present phonologically in Ukrainian.

Issues in Metrical Phonology

,σσ'σσ,σ   [,pɔpɛ'rɛdnʲɔ,ɦɔ] 'previous, gen. sg. masc.'
,σσσ'σσ   [,lʲitɛra'tura] 'literature, nom. sg.'
,σσ,σσ'σ   [,unʲi,ʋɛrsi'tɛt] 'university, nom. sg.'

d. *Six-syllable words*
'σσσ,σσ,σ   ['batʃiti,mɛtɛ,sʲa] 'see, 2nd pers. pl. refl. future'
σ'σσ,σσ,σ   [ʋɨ'xɔdi,timɛ,mɔ] 'go out, 1st pers. pl. future'
,σσ'σσσ,σ   [,nafɔ'lɔʃuʋa,nnʲa] 'accenting, nom. sg.'
,σσσ'σσ,σ   [,zarɔzu'mʲilʲi,stʲu] 'conceit, instr. sg.'
,σσ,σσ'σσ   [,pɔdɔ,rɔʒu'ʋala] 'travel, 3rd pers. sg. fem. past'
,σσ,σσσ'σ   [,munʲi,t͡sipalʲi'tɛt] 'municipality, nom. sg.'

e. *Seven-syllable words*
'σσ,σσ,σσ,σ   ['ʋiba,lansu,ʋati,sʲa] 'balance out, inf. perf.'
σ'σσσ,σσ,σ   [za'pamɔrɔ,t͡ʃɛnnʲa,mɨ] 'dizziness, instr. pl.'
,σσ'σσ,σσ,σ   [,pɛrɛ'ʋiʃt͡ʃu,ʋati,mutʲ] 'exceed, 3rd pers. pl. future'
,σσσ'σσσ,σ   [,ʋikɔri'stɔʋuʋa,nnʲa] 'usage, nom. sg.'
,σσ,σσ'σσ,σ   [,admʲi,nʲistra'tiʋnɔ,mu] 'administrative, dat. sg. masc.'
,σσ,σσσ'σσ   [,kapʲi,talʲizu'ʋati] 'capitalise, inf.'
,σσ,σσ,σσ'σ   [,intɛr,nat͡sʲi,ɔna'lʲizm] 'internationalism, nom. sg.'

These examples show that while lexical stress can appear on any syllable, the position of secondary stress is predictable. Initial and final syllables have secondary prominence when not immediately followed or preceded by lexical stress – for example, the initial syllable is stressed in ,σσσ'σσ [,lʲitɛra'tura] 'literature, nom. sg.' and the final syllable is stressed in σ'σσσ,σ [kɔm'panʲijɛ,ju] 'company, instr. sg.'. In contrast, the initial syllable in [kɔm'panʲijɛ,ju] and the final syllable in [,lʲitɛra'tura] remain unstressed because they are adjacent to lexical stress. Furthermore, word-medial rhythmic stress appears in longer words, in which lexical stress is removed from the left or the right word edge by four or more syllables, for example, ,σσ,σσ'σσ [,pɔdɔ,rɔʒu'ʋala] 'travel, 3rd pers. sg. fem. past', σ'σσ,σσ,σ [ʋɨ'xɔdi,timɛ,mɔ] 'go out, 1st pers. pl. future', with a lapse occurring next to lexical stress, for example, ,σσ,σσσ'σσ [,munʲi,t͡sipalʲi'tɛt] 'municipality, nom. sg.', 'σσσ,σσ,σ ['batʃiti,mɛtɛ,sʲa] 'see, 2nd pers. pl. refl. future '.

It has been previously noted that Ukrainian is a highly inflectional language with complex morphology. Derived environments are notorious for their interaction with stress assignment in a number of languages. An illustrative example comes from English, in which secondary stress is lexicalised and its location is often unpredictable. For instance, the initial syllable is stressed in ,characte'ristic because its derivational base is 'character, a word with initial primary stress. In contrast, the word A,meri'cana has secondary stress on the second syllable because it is derived from A'merica, in which the second syllable carries metrical prominence (Chomsky & Halle 1968; Hayes 1980; Halle & Vergnaud 1987). Unlike English, Ukrainian does not exhibit interactions between morphological structure and secondary stress placement (Łukaszewicz & Mołczanow 2018b; Mołczanow & Łukaszewicz 2021). The evidence provided in Mołczanow and Łukaszewicz (2021: 556–557) is based on the regular distribution of secondary prominence in unaccented stems and on alternations such as [xaˈraktɛr] 'character, nom. sg.' – [ˌxaraktɛˈristiˌka] 'characteristics, nom. sg.', in which the location of the lexical stress in the base [xaˈraktɛr] does not align with the position of the secondary stress in the derived form [ˌxaraktɛˈristiˌka]. It is also notable that, unlike primary stress, secondary stress is not marked in dictionaries of Ukrainian. Furthermore, native speakers do not have intuitions as to its presence or location within a word, which renders rhythmic stress in Ukrainian similar to languages such as Polish, in which the regular distribution of grammatical stress is independent of the morphological structure (Rubach & Booij 1985; Kraska-Szlenk 2003; Łukaszewicz 2018).

2.1.2 A Phonological Model of the Ukrainian Metrical System

As introduced in Section 1.2, the Ukrainian rhythmic pattern is reminiscent of typologically rare bidirectional stress systems with internal lapses (Łukaszewicz & Mołczanow 2018a, 2018b, 2019; Mołczanow & Łukaszewicz 2021). In such systems, main stress is fixed with respect to the right or left edge of the word, while rhythmic stresses iterate from the opposite edge; compare Kager (2001) and Gordon (2002). The iteration of (feet containing) rhythmic stress thus proceeds either from the word's beginning rightwards (e.g. [(ˌσσ)(ˌσσ)σ(ˈσσ)], not *[σ(ˌσσ)(ˌσσ)(ˈσσ)], as in Polish; Rubach & Booij 1985; Kraska-Szlenk 2003; Łukaszewicz 2015, 2018; Łukaszewicz et al. 2018, 2020) or from the word's end leftwards (e.g. [(ˈσσ)σ(ˌσσ)(ˌσσ)], not *[(ˈσσ)(ˌσσ)σ(ˌσσ)], as in Garawa; Furby (1974), cited, for example, in Gordon (2002) and Kager (2005). Stress clashes are avoided – when there is an odd number of syllables between the word's edge and the main stress position, a lapse (i.e. a sequence of two unstressed syllables) occurs in the vicinity of main stress.

Classical bidirectional stress systems such as Polish or Garawa are purely grammatical metrical systems – in such systems, (feet containing) primary and secondary stresses both occur at word edges. As a consequence, the only possibility admitted within a single system is that of secondary stresses iterating from one edge, which is the opposite edge with respect to the one where primary stress occurs (Łukaszewicz et al. submitted). Similarly to those previously known bidirectional systems, Ukrainian exhibits rhythmic stress propagation from the word's edge towards the main stress position (Łukaszewicz &

Mołczanow 2018a, 2018b). However, unlike those systems, Ukrainian has free lexical stress, which can occur in any position in the word. As highlighted in Section 2.1.1, this gives rise to a large number of possible combinations of primary and secondary (rhythmic) prominences, depending on the position of lexical stress relative to the word edges. As a consequence, there can be simultaneously rightward and leftward rhythmic stress iteration in Ukrainian, starting off at both edges (Łukaszewicz & Mołczanow 2018a, 2018b). In what follows, we discuss the challenge that this characteristic of the Ukrainian system poses to current metrical theories designed for simpler, purely grammatical stress systems (Łukaszewicz & Mołczanow 2019; Mołczanow & Łukaszewicz 2021). The discussion will focus on three- and six-syllable words – the former have the minimal length to accommodate two levels of stress; the latter have sufficient length to exhibit rhythmic stress iteration and a lapse at the peak, which makes Ukrainian a bidirectional stress system.

In order to accommodate rhythmic stress, the word minimally needs to consist of three syllables. In (3), we repeat for convenience all possible combinations of lexical and rhythmic stress on the basis of three-syllable words, illustrated earlier in (2a). Lexical stress falls on the first syllable in (3a), second syllable in (3b), and third syllable in (3c). In general, rhythmic stress is placed on the initial or final syllable of the word if at least one syllable intervenes between that syllable and the one carrying lexical stress. Thus, it is present in (3a) and (3c), in which the lexically stressed and the rhythmically stressed syllables occupy the opposite edges, but not in (3b), in which the lexically stressed syllable occurs in the middle of the word. The stress pattern in (3c) is a mirror image with respect to the one in (3a).

(3) *Possible rhythmic stress patterns in three-syllable words*
    a. [ˈσσˌσ] b. [σˈσσ] c. [ˌσσˈσ]

Three-syllable words are too short to accommodate rhythmic stress iteration, which can only be found in longer words. For rhythmic stress iteration to occur, at least four syllables should intervene between the word's edge and the lexical stress position, which means that the minimal length of the word must be that of five syllables. However, the presence of iterative stress does not automatically indicate that the pattern is unidirectional or bidirectional. In 'even-parity' words – that is, words having an even number of syllables between the word's edge and the lexical stress position, for example, [ˈσσˌσσˌσ] or [ˌσσˌσσˈσ], compare (2c) – the metrical structures are non-transparent with regard to the direction of rhythmic stress propagation: such structures may arise through rhythmic beats propagating from the lexical stress position towards the edge (as in a unidirectional pattern) or in the opposite direction (as in a bidirectional pattern), yielding practically the same results. A key argument for stress bidirectionality is then the position of a lapse in 'odd-parity' words. This can be illustrated by looking at possible combinations of lexical and rhythmic stress in six-syllable words in (4) (cf. (2d)). In bidirectional stress systems, the lapse is located near the peak, as schematised in (4a) and (4f). In those examples, the distance between the edge and the lexical stress position is that of five syllables, which allows us to infer both the iterative and bidirectional character of rhythmic stress in Ukrainian. In (4a), the structure is [ˈσσσˌσσˌσ], with a lapse located at the peak, not [ˈσσˌσσσˌσ], with a lapse occurring between rhythmic stresses, and also not *[ˈσσˌσσˌσσ] with no lapse at all and no rhythmic stress on the final syllable. The metrical structure in (4f), which is [ˌσσˌσσσˈσ], is a mirror image of the one in (4a); analogously to (4a), it reflects the bidirectional characteristics of the Ukrainian system.

(4) *Possible rhythmic stress patterns in six-syllable words*
 a. [ˈσσσˌσσˌσ]
 b. [σˈσσˌσσˌσ]
 c. [ˌσσˈσσσˌσ]
 d. [ˌσσσˈσσˌσ]
 e. [ˌσσˌσσˈσσ]
 f. [ˌσσˌσσσˈσ]

In what follows, we discuss the theoretical implications of the existence of mirror-image stress patterns such as [ˈσσˌσ] (3a) versus [ˌσσˈσ] (3c) and [ˈσσσˌσσˌσ] (4a) versus [ˌσσˌσσσˈσ] (4f) within a single stress system. In Section 2.2, we will present the results of recent acoustic studies which corroborate the bidirectional characteristics of the metrical system of Ukrainian, but also point to some additional adjustments affecting the phonetic manifestation of metrical stress. Specifically, it will be shown that vowels in pretonic positions (i.e. positions immediately preceding lexical stress) exhibit increased duration. The effect of pretonic lengthening interferes with the otherwise regular rhythmic stress pattern, causing it to disappear in the vicinity of lexical stress. We further argue in Section 3 of this Element that pretonic lengthening can be viewed as an extended lexical stress domain effect, formally modelled in terms of grid-based representations.

As briefly discussed in Section 1.2, contemporary metrical theories provide various tools for describing classical bidirectional stress systems with internal lapses (e.g. Rubach & Booij 1985; McCarthy & Prince 1993; van der Hulst 1996, 2012, 2014; Kager 2001, 2005; Gordon 2002; Hyde 2002, 2016; Alber 2005). These tools differ in whether they are based on rules, output constraints, or parameters; they also differ in assumptions concerning the representation of stress – that is, whether it should be grid-based and/or foot-based. Most of the previous accounts are couched in the constraint-based framework of Optimality Theory (OT), regulating the positioning of stress in terms of alignment constraints. Alignment constraints require that the designated (left or right) edge of some prosodic domain coincide with the corresponding edge of some other prosodic or morphological domain (McCarthy & Prince 1993). They can be either categorical (Kager 2001, 2005) or gradient (McCarthy & Prince 1993; Alber 2005).

The attraction of rhythmic stress to the word edges in three-syllable words in (3a) and (3c) can be modelled in a straightforward way in terms of a high-ranking categorical alignment constraint, ALIGN EDGES (Gordon 2002: 497). Assuming the grid-based approach of Gordon (2002), ALIGN EDGES requires that the edges of level 0 of a prosodic word – that is, the level corresponding to syllable positions – be aligned with a grid mark on level 1 – that is, the level corresponding to rhythmic stress (5). Words having the structure (5a) or (5c) fully satisfy this constraint because both the initial and the final syllable align with grid marks on level 1 in those words, and, additionally, no violation of *CLASH ensues. *CLASH is based on a rhythmic principle proposed by Prince (1983), which prohibits adjacent stressed syllables within a given stress domain; with reference to the metrical grid, it can be formulated as '[a]djacent syllables carrying a level 1 grid mark are banned' (Gordon 2002: 506). The grid marks on level 1 in lexically stressed syllables appear through extrapolation of level 2 – that is, the level corresponding to primary stress. Example (5b) violates ALIGN EDGES twice; however, it remains the optimal structure because of its stress clash avoidance, as enforced by the domination of *CLASH. This analysis is summarised in Table 2. Following standard practice, underlying representations are given in slashes.

(5) *Grid representations of three-syllable words differing in the position of lexical stress*

a. [ˈσσˌσ]	b. [σˈσσ]	c. [ˌσσˈσ]	
x .	x	. x	level 2 (primary stress)
x . x	. x .	x . x	level 1 (secondary stress)
σ σ σ	σ σ σ	σ σ σ	level 0 (syllable positions)
[ˈdɔrɔˌfiɔ]	[dɔˈrɔfia]	[ˌdɔrɔˈfia]	
'expensive, adv.'	'way, nom. sg.'	'dear, nom. sg. fem.'	

More problematic from the theoretical point of view is the accommodation of the mirror-image stress patterns in six-syllable words: [ˈσσσˌσσˌσ] (4a) versus [ˌσσˌσσσˈσ] (4f). Basically, there are two theoretical approaches which can be employed to guarantee the occurrence of a lapse near the peak in

Table 2 Grid-based approach with categorical alignment: three-syllable words

	*CLASH	ALIGN EDGES
a. /ˈdɔrɔfiɔ/		
⇒ i. ˈdɔrɔˌfiɔ		
ii. ˈdɔˌrɔfiɔ	*!	*
iii. ˈdɔrɔfiɔ		*!
b. /dɔˈrɔfia/		
⇒ i. dɔˈrɔfia		**
ii. ˌdɔˈrɔfia	*!	*
c. /dɔrɔˈfia/		
⇒ i. ˌdɔrɔˈfia		*
ii. dɔˌrɔˈfia	*!	*
iii. dɔrɔˈfia		*!

bidirectional stress systems: gradient alignment versus licencing. The former will have an effect of pushing rhythmic stresses towards the left or the right edge of the word; a by-product of this effect will be creating a lapse either to the left or to the right of primary stress in 'odd-parity' words, depending on the designated edge in the alignment constraint. The latter, by admitting marked structures such as lapses in the vicinity of certain prosodic positions, here primary stress, will have a general effect of repelling rhythmic stresses away from the lexical stress position. As we discuss in what follows, the limitations of the gradient alignment mechanism are immediately clear in a system where rhythmic stress propagation should occur in both directions simultaneously. This is so regardless of whether grid-only or foot-based representations are assumed. The licencing mechanism allows us to generate correct predictions for the rhythmic stress patterns in the Ukrainian system, but only when it operates on grid-based, not foot-based representations.

Gradient alignment constraints can be multiply violated, depending on the distance (the number of syllable units) separating the designated edges of two domains. In what follows, we illustrate the problem posed by the Ukrainian pattern, assuming a foot-based gradient alignment approach (McCarthy & Prince 1993; Alber 2005), in which syllables are parsed into binary left-headed (trochaic) or right-headed (iambic) feet. The operational effect of gradient alignment is that all feet containing rhythmic stresses are pushed either to the left or to the right, depending on the mutual ranking of the alignment constraint ALIGN-FT-L ('the left edge of every foot is aligned with the left edge of prosodic word'; McCarthy &

Table 3 Foot-based approach with gradient alignment:
ALIGN-FT-L ≫ ALIGN-FT-R

	ALIGN-FT-L	ALIGN-FT-R
a. rightward iteration		
⇒ i. (ˌmunʲi)(ˌt͡sɨpa)lʲi(ˈtɛt)	** (2), (*****)	**, **** (6)
ii. (ˌmunʲi)t͡sɨ(ˌpalʲi)(ˈtɛt)	***! (3), (*****)	*, **** (5)
iii. mu(ˌnʲit͡sɨ)(ˌpalʲi)(ˈtɛt)	*, **!* (4), (*****)	*, *** (4)
b. leftward iteration		
☺ i. (ˈlafiɔ)dɨ (ˌtimɛ)(ˌtɛ)	***, ****!* (8)	* (1), (****)
ii. (ˈlafiɔ)(ˌdɨtɨ)mɛ(ˌtɛ)	**, *****! (7)	** (2), (****)
⇐ iii. (ˈlafiɔ)(ˌdɨtɨ)(ˌmɛtɛ)	**, **** (6)	** (2), (****)

Prince 1993) and ALIGN-FT-R ('the right edge of every foot is aligned with the right edge of prosodic word'; McCarthy & Prince 1993). As shown in Table 3 (based on Mołczanow & Łukaszewicz 2021: 559), if ALIGN-FT-L is ranked above ALIGN-FT-R, then secondary stress is assigned from the left word edge, correctly generating the rightward stress iteration in [ˌmunʲi ˌt͡sɨpalʲ ˈtɛt] in (a) but incorrectly deriving penultimate secondary stress in *[ˈlafiɔˌdɨtɨˌmɛtɛ] in (b). In turn, the correct form [ˈlafiɔdɨˌtimɛˌtɛ] and the erroneous output *[muˌnʲit͡sɨˌpalʲiˈtɛt] are generated by the reverse ranking ALIGN-FT-R ≫ ALIGN-FT-L. An arbitrary parsing into trochaic rather than iambic feet is assumed in this analysis; also it is far from clear under what conditions unary feet would be allowed in Ukrainian. It is important to add that the gradient alignment mechanism fails to generate the rightward and leftward stress iteration simultaneously also when it operates in terms of prominence marks on the grid rather than in terms of feet. Thus, replacing ALIGN-FT-L and ALIGN-FT-R with ALIGN (x1, L) and ALIGN (x1, R), which require that every level 1 grid mark be aligned with the left/right edge of level 0 of grid marks in a prosodic word (see Gordon 2002), would essentially lead to the same directionality paradoxes. Let us also observe that, unlike in the simpler case of three-syllable words schematised in Table 2, the directionality paradox in the longer words in Table 3 cannot be resolved in terms of *CLASH ≫ ALIGN EDGES, because this sub-hierarchy of constraints treats competing outputs, such as [(ˌσσ)(ˌσσ) σ (ˈσ)] vs. [(ˌσσ)σ(ˌσσ)(ˈσ)] as well as [(ˈσσ)σ(ˌσσ)(ˌσ)] versus [(ˈσσ)(ˌσσ)σ(ˌσ)] as faring equally well.

An alternative mechanism is that of licencing, which admits rhythmically marked entities (lapses) in a limited set of prosodic positions (the peak and the right edge of the prosodic domain); see Kager (2001, 2005). This is

Table 4 Foot-based approach with categorical alignment and licencing

	ALIGN-WD-L	ALIGN-WD-R	LAPSE-AT-PEAK	*LAPSE
a. rightward iteration				
⇒ i. (ˌmunʲi)(ˌt͡sipa)lʲi(ˈtɛt)				*
ii. (ˌmunʲi)t͡si(ˌpalʲi)(ˈtɛt)			*!	*
iii. mu(ˌnʲit͡si)(ˌpalʲi)(ˈtɛt)	*!			
b. leftward iteration				
☺ i. (ˈlafɔ)dɨ(ˌtimɛ)(ˌtɛ)				*!
ii. (ˈlafɔ)(ˌditɨ)mɛ(ˌtɛ)			*!	*
⇐ iii. (ˈlafɔ)(ˌditɨ)(ˌmɛtɛ)				

achieved by a licencing rhythmic constraint, LAPSE-AT-PEAK ('Lapse must be adjacent to the peak'; Kager 2001: 4). To generate edge-based stress, the model employs categorical constraints ALIGN-WD-L and ALIGN-WD-R ('every prosodic word starts/ends with a foot'; Kager 2001). There are two insurmountable problems that this model encounters. First, as it operates on feet, it faces the same problem of arbitrary foot assignment as the model based on gradient alignment (McCarthy & Prince 1993; Alber 2005): the initial stress derives from locating a trochaic foot at a left word edge, whereas the final stress is modelled by building a unary foot at the right edge of the word. Like the model in Table 3, it can derive either word-initial or word-final secondary stress, but not both.[5] Table 4 serves to illustrate the point (based on Mołczanow & Łukaszewicz 2021: 561). The correct output [(ˈlafɔ)dɨ(ˌtimɛ) (ˌtɛ)] in (bi) is suboptimal relative to the fully parsed candidate [(ˈlafɔ)(ˌditɨ) (ˌmɛtɛ)] in (biii).

It has been pointed out in Mołczanow and Łukaszewicz (2021) that it is possible to construct an alternative foot-based analysis if the increased duration of stressed syllables is encoded phonologically. In this model, bimoraic vowels in metrically strong positions are opposed to monomoraic unstressed vowels, and bimoraic feet are built for both lexically and rhythmically stressed syllables, as shown in Figure 1. Edge-based stress is derived by constructing bimoraic feet at both word edges, which is achieved by means of the constraints ALIGN-WD-L and ALIGN-WD-R, whereas bidirectional iterative stress is derived by the

---

[5] Other models proposed in the literature which could potentially be used in the analysis of Ukrainian include Hyde's (2002) model assuming intersected feet and Martínez-Paricio and Kager's (2015) model postulating internally layered binary and ternary feet. As we extensively argue in Mołczanow and Łukaszewicz (2021), these analyses are equally unsuccessful in dealing with the Ukrainian data as they run into the same contradictions as the classical foot-based models discussed earlier in this Element.

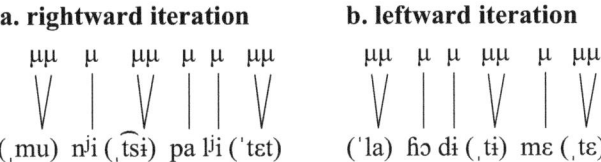

Figure 1 Approach employing moraic feet.

licencing constraint LAPSE-AT-PEAK, as in the foot-based licencing approach with categorical alignment illustrated in Table 4.

Although this analysis can technically derive the Ukrainian pattern, it is problematic for several reasons. First, it assumes a two-way length contrast in vowels which does not express a lexical contrast and thus serves a diacritic purpose, its function being merely the identification of the location of secondary prominence. Another objection concerns the consequences of this assumption for the modelling of the phonological processes of Ukrainian unconnected to stress. In particular, Mołczanow and Łukaszewicz (2021) demonstrate that the phonological distinction in vocalic duration (one mora vs. two moras) complicates the analysis of glides and geminates in Ukrainian. As for the former, the glides [j] and [w] alternate with high vowels [i] and [u] at word boundaries – for example, [ˈvʲin iˈdɛ] 'he goes' – [vɔˈna ˈjdɛ] 'she goes', [iˈdutʲ uˈt͡ʃiti̯sʲa] 'they go to study' – [iˈdu ˈwt͡ʃiti̯sʲa] 'I go to study' (Toc'ka 2002). This process interacts with moraic structure because gliding, which is used to resolve vowel hiatus and thus improve syllable structure, consists in a loss of a mora. Mołczanow and Łukaszewicz (2021) argue that the analysis assuming bimoraic feet incorrectly predicts that the vowel would be deleted, not glided, when preceded by either lexically or rhythmically stressed syllable – for example, the model would generate an incorrect form *[ˈlit͡sa̯ˌrʲi ˈdutʲ] instead of the attested [ˈlit͡sa̯ˌrʲi ˈjdutʲ] 'knights go' (see Mołczanow & Łukaszewicz 2021: 570–572 for further discussion).

Another argument against bimoraic feet adduced in Mołczanow and Łukaszewicz (2021) comes from the phonology of geminate consonants. Long (geminate) consonants contrast with single consonants in Ukrainian – for example, [ˈlʲutʲ] 'rage, nom. sg.' – [ˈlʲlʲutʲ] 'pour, 3rd pers. pl. pres.', [suˈdʲi] 'court, loc. sg.' – [suˈddʲi] 'judge, gen. sg.', [ˈsinʲu] 'blue, adj. fem. acc. sg.' – [ˈsinnʲu] 'blue, noun instr. sg.' (Toc'ka 1969; Bethin 1992; Loboda 2009). Geminates are standardly encoded in the underlying representation as moraic, whereas single consonants are underlyingly moraless (Hayes 1989). Assuming that stressed syllables are bimoraic and geminate consonants are moraic (as

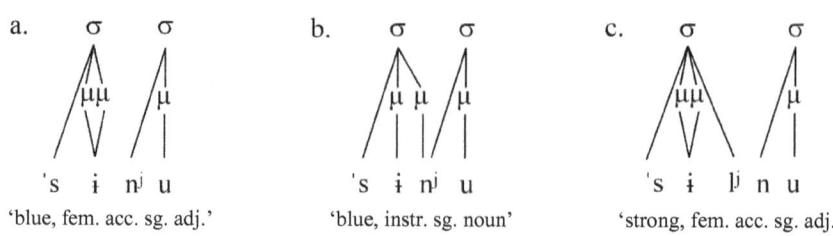

Figure 2 Moraic representation of a word-medial (a) singleton, (b) geminate, (c) cluster.

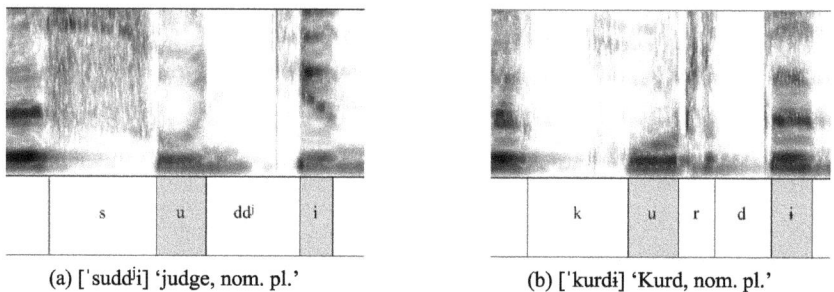

Figure 3 An illustration of comparable vowel duration before (a) a geminate and (b) a cluster.

illustrated in Figure 2), the model predicts stressed vowels to be shorter before geminate consonants (Mołczanow & Łukaszewicz 2021: 570).

Though shortening of vowels before geminates is not uncommon cross-linguistically (consider e.g. Italian; Krämer 2009), no such differences have been reported in the literature on Ukrainian and our preliminary study has not revealed any differences either. As illustrated in Figure 3, the duration of the vowel [u] is comparable in the words [ˈsuddʲi] 'judge, nom. pl.' and [ˈkurdɨ] 'Kurd, nom. pl' (102 ms vs. 101 ms, respectively).

In sum, the Ukrainian data cannot be accounted for using a mechanism relying on feet. As argued extensively in Mołczanow and Łukaszewicz (2021), neither gradient alignment (McCarthy & Prince 1993) nor categorical alignment coupled with foot-based licencing constraints (Kager 2001) can successfully derive the Ukrainian system, because these mechanisms would push all rhythmic stresses either to the left or to the right, independent of whether the assumed foot type is binary or ternary (Martínez-Paricio & Kager 2015; see also fn. 2). Mołczanow and Łukaszewicz (2021) further argue that the Ukrainian data provide strong support for a grid-based representation, as advocated in Gordon (2002). In this model, edge-based stress is generated by the constraint ALIGN EDGES ('Every grid mark of level 1 is aligned with the {right, left} edge of level 0 of grid marks in a prosodic word'; Gordon 2002: 497). ALIGN EDGES thus aligns the initial and final syllables with a grid mark on a prosodic level corresponding to secondary stress, as illustrated in (6). (The same constraint was used in our analysis of the rhythmic stress pattern, summarised in Table 2.) The location of word-medial (iterative) rhythmic stresses is predicted by gradient alignment constraints ALIGN (x1, L) and ALIGN (x1, R) in Gordon's (2002) approach. As pointed out previously in this Element, although these constraints are defined in terms of a metrical grid, they lead to the same directionality paradoxes as foot-based gradient alignment because they enforce aligning the grid marks on level 1 with the left or right edge of the word, but not both. As such, they yield incorrect predictions for the rhythmic stress iteration patterns in Ukrainian and cannot predict the position of lapses in the examples in (6).

(6) *Grid representations for six-syllable words with bidirectional rhythmic stress*

```
         x              x            Level 2 (primary stress)
   x . x . . x    x . . x . x        Level 1 (secondary stress)
   x x x x x x    x x x x x x        Level 0 (syllable positions)
   ˌmunʲi ts͡ipalʲi'tɛt  'lafiɔdɨˌtimɛˌtɛ
```

To derive both lapses in the vicinity of lexical stress, Mołczanow and Łukaszewicz (2021) employ the licencing constraint LAPSE-AT-PEAK ('Lapse must be adjacent to the peak'; Kager 2001: 4), as in the foot-based approach with categorical alignment and licencing; cf. Table 4). Combining the grid-based constraint ALIGN EDGES with the licencing constraint LAPSE-AT-PEAK allows for a successful generation of the Ukrainian pattern, as illustrated by the evaluation shown in Table 5 (Mołczanow & Łukaszewicz 2021: 567).

It is evident, then, that the metrical theory can in principle model the bidirectional iterative stress system of Ukrainian. However, as we will see in the remainder of this Element, this regular pattern of alternating rhythmic stresses is an idealisation which is not instantiated phonetically in an unambiguous way. Whereas the acoustic correlates of lexical stress are robust, the distinction between vowels carrying secondary stress and unstressed vowels is not always explicitly manifested in the acoustic signal. We will see that there exist significant phonetic differences between the stressed and unstressed vowels located to the left and to the right of lexical stress. Namely, syllables preceding lexical stress in ˌσσˈσ(σ) and ˌσσσˈσ(σ) show a gradual increase in duration from the left word edge towards lexical stress. This pattern of pretonic lengthening obliterates the duration-based expression of initial rhythmic stress. In what follows, we tackle the asymmetry between pretonic and posttonic

Table 5 A combination of the grid-based approach and the licencing approach

	ALIGN EDGES	LAPSE-AT-PEAK
a. rightward iteration		
⇒ i. ˌmunʲiˌt͡sɨpalʲiˈtɛt		
ii. ˌmunʲit͡sɨˌpalʲiˈtɛt		*!
iii. muˌnʲit͡sɨˌpalʲiˈtɛt	*!	
b. leftward iteration		
⇒ i. ˈlaɦɔdɨˌtimɛˌtɛ		
ii. ˈlaɦɔˌdɨtimɛˌtɛ		*!
iii. ˈlaɦɔˌdɨtɨˌmɛtɛ	*!	

positions in a series of acoustic studies based on words having different length. We investigate how the varying distance between the right/left word edge and lexical stress affects the phonetic manifestation of rhythmic stress and other prosodic phenomena. We also propose an extension of the model combining the grid-based approach and the licencing approach to account for the asymmetry between pretonic and posttonic position. Novel data are synthesised with those reported in previous studies to improve our understanding of the interaction between the lexical and grammatical stress domains, as well as the potential interaction between stress-related and other (e.g. positional) factors.

2.2 Acoustic Correlates of Ukrainian Stress

2.2.1 Lexical Stress

As demonstrated by previous findings (e.g. Łukaszewicz & Mołczanow 2018a, 2018b, 2018c), stress is manifested acoustically in terms of increased syllable/vowel duration in Ukrainian. Some authors single out intensity as a correlate of lexical stress in Ukrainian (Nakonečnyj 1969: 359; Brovčenko 1969; Loboda 2009: 21); however, acoustic measurements presented in Łukaszewicz and Mołczanow (2018c) demonstrate that intensity and F0 are not employed to cue word-level prominence. Numerous recent studies based on polysyllabic words of different length and with different primary stress location (e.g. Łukaszewicz & Mołczanow 2018a, 2018b, 2018c; Mołczanow *et al.* 2018, 2021) point to robust differences between lexically stressed syllables/vowels and those in metrically weak positions. Lexically stressed syllables are reported to be nearly 2 times longer than unstressed syllables in Łukaszewicz and Mołczanow's (2018a) study, based on syllable duration measurements in five- and six-syllable words with lexical stress on the initial syllable, such as

[ˈbat͡ʃɨˌtimɛˌtɛ] 'see, 2nd pers. pl. future' (p. 266). In another study (Łukaszewicz & Mołczanow 2018b), based on words with lexical stress on the final syllable or near the end of the word – that is, on the fourth, fifth, and sixth syllables, as in [ˌʋɛlɔsɨˈpɛdnɨj] 'bicycle, nom. sg. adj.', [ˌɔrfiaˌnʲizuˈʋatɨ] 'organise, inf.', [ˌkapʲiˌtalʲizuˈʋatɨ] 'capitalise, inf.', lexically stressed syllables are 1.5 times longer than other syllables within a word (p. 380). In absolute terms, those stress-dependent differences are reported to be 86 ms for the low vowel /a/ and 49 ms for high vowels, on the basis of words with lexical stress on the fifth syllable (Łukaszewicz & Mołczanow 2018c: 373). In a study of minimal pairs, which differ only in terms of the position of lexical stress – for example, [pɔˈpadaˌti] 'fall, inf. perf.' – [ˌpɔpaˈdatɨ] 'strike and hit the mark, inf. imperf.), the average difference between the vowels in the corresponding lexical versus unstressed position in the third syllable is 83 ms; the lexically stressed vowels turn out 2.3 times longer than the unstressed ones (Mołczanow *et al.* 2021: 11).

2.2.2 Rhythmic Stress

The presence of rhythmic stress has been reported in traditional descriptive grammars of Ukrainian (Broch 1910; Lehr-Spławiński 1916; Ziłyński 1932; Bilodid 1969); its acoustic correlates have been recently studied in a number of experiments (Łukaszewicz & Mołczanow 2018a *et seq.*). Similarly to lexical stress, rhythmic stress is expressed by increased duration. However, although rhythmically stressed and unstressed syllables differ in length, the difference between them is much smaller compared to the difference in the lexical stress contexts. In addition, rhythmic stress is an optional phenomenon, with different speakers showing different levels of rhythmicity (e.g. Łukaszewicz & Mołczanow 2018a; Mołczanow *et al.* 2021).

Studies of both the leftward and rightward stress iteration in Ukrainian have been conducted. The leftward rhythmic stress iteration has been investigated on the basis of words with lexical stress on the initial syllable, having the structure [ˈσσˌσσˌσ] or [ˈσσσˌσσˌσ] (Łukaszewicz & Mołczanow 2018a). The analysis of more than 2,100 syllable tokens from twelve speakers reveals consistent lengthening of the final syllable and optional lengthening of the third syllable from the end in such words. On the basis of segmentally identical syllables, a statistically significant increase of 16 ms is reported in the iterative stress position in comparison with the preceding unstressed syllable, which is part of a lapse in [ˈσσσˌσσˌσ] words. Similar results have been obtained for words with the rightward iteration. In Łukaszewicz & Mołczanow's (2018b) study, based on acoustic measurements in more than 1,400 syllable tokens from sixteen speakers, the initial syllable is on average 30 ms longer than the second

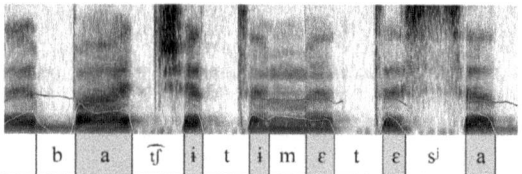

['baˀʃiti ˌmɛtɛ ˌsʲa] 'see, 2nd pers. refl. pl. future'

Figure 4 Leftward rhythmic stress iteration.

syllable in [ˌσσσˈσ(σ)], [ˌσσˌσσˈσ(σ)], and [ˌσσˌσσσˈσ(σ)] words. (Duration measurements were conducted on the basis of whole syllables in that study.) A significant increase in duration is also reported for the iterative position (the third syllable) in [ˌσσˌσσˈσ(σ)], and [ˌσσˌσσσˈσ(σ)] words, which turns out 21 ms longer than the preceding (i.e. second) metrically weak syllable. In another analysis based on segmentally identical syllables in words with potential stress iteration, the iterative position (third syllable) is about 16 ms longer than the preceding unstressed syllable, with a statistically significant effect of rhythmic stress (p. 379).

In sum, we can infer from the temporal patterns present in the acoustic speech signal that rhythmic stress propagation in Ukrainian proceeds as predicted for bidirectional systems – that is, from the word's edge towards the main stress position, with lapses occurring near the peak. The presence of edge-based rhythmic stress propagation is illustrated in Figure 4, which depicts the metrical pattern in a word with lexical stress on the initial syllable, [ˈbaʧiti ˌmɛtɛ ˌsʲa] 'see, 2nd pers. refl. pl. future'. A conspicuous durational effect is seen in the lexically stressed syllable; also, the rhythmically stressed syllables exhibit longer vowels compared to those in adjacent unstressed syllables. This example clearly demonstrates the leftward direction of rhythmic stress propagation – the lapse formed by the sequence -ʧiti- is clearly located at the peak.

Figure 5 illustrates the metrical patterns in words with lexical stress on the fifth (a), and sixth syllables (b). Both in [ˌkataˌlʲizuˈvati] 'catalyse, inf.' (a) and [ˌtɛlɛˌfɔnʲizuˈvati] 'to set up a telephone connection, inf.' (b), the lexically stressed vowel in the syllable -va- is clearly the longest of all. In accordance with the bidirectional system's characteristics, here we expect rhythmic stress iteration in the reversed direction – from the word's beginning rightwards, which is indeed the case. In both examples, the vowel in the initial (rhythmically stressed) syllable is longer than the vowel in the second (unstressed) syllable. The third (rhythmically stressed) syllable is slightly enhanced in comparison with the preceding syllable. Altogether, the expected [ˌσσˌσ-] pattern appears across the first three syllables in those words. However, there also seems to be

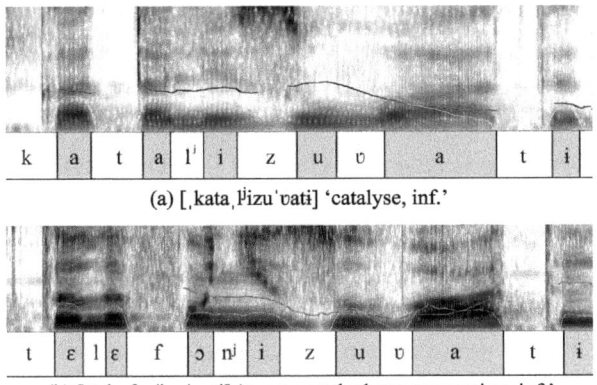

Figure 5 Rightward rhythmic stress iteration – durational enhancement of vowels in the rhythmically stressed initial and third syllables; pretonic lengthening of the vowel in the fourth syllable in (a) and the fourth and fifth syllables in (b).

an extra domain of temporal enhancement in the syllables preceding lexical stress, visible in Figure 5, which we address in Section 2.2.3.

2.2.3 Pretonic Lengthening

We can infer from both Figure 4 and Figure 5 that rhythmic stress applies at the left/right edge and iterates towards the position of main stress; the rightward pattern [ˌσσˌσ-] thus seems to be a mirror image of the leftward pattern [-ˌσσˌσ]. However, by comparing the two figures, we may also observe that this symmetrical bidirectional characteristic of the Ukrainian system is not fully reified on the physical level. There is no perfect symmetry in the temporal patterns to the immediate left and to the immediate right of lexical stress. In Figure 5, there seems to be increased duration in the pretonic syllable relative to the rhythmically stressed vowels in the initial and third syllables. No such duration enhancement is seen in the posttonic syllable in Figure 4 – the vowel in the posttonic position seems to be conspicuously shorter than the rhythmically stressed vowels in the antepenultimate and final syllables.

The presence of an extra domain of temporal enhancement in the syllable immediately preceding the position of lexical stress was observed in previous studies of the Ukrainian metrical system; the phenomenon has been referred to as 'pretonic lengthening' (Łukaszewicz & Mołczanow 2018b, 2018c; Mołczanow *et al.* 2019b). Comparisons of vocalic duration in different prosodic positions in words with lexical stress on the fifth syllable (i.e. words having the structure [ˌσσˌσσˈσ(σ)]) showed that vowels are on average 14 ms longer in the pretonic position than in the unstressed (second) position (Łukaszewicz & Mołczanow 2018c). Acoustic measurements demonstrate that pretonic lengthening is consistently present across various types of words – that is, also in words where no rhythmic stress iteration is expected. In a recent systematic study of the pretonic lengthening effect in Ukrainian (Łukaszewicz *et al.* submitted), based on words with lexical stress on the fourth syllable (i.e. words having the structure [ˌσσσˈσ(σ)]), pretonic vowels exceed in length both the vowels in the rhythmically stressed (initial) and the unstressed (second) position. The statistically significant difference between the vowel /a/ in the pretonic and the initial position amounts to 10 ms. As we will see in Sections 2.2.4 and 2.3.2, an increase in duration is also observed in the pretonic syllable in shorter quadri- and tri-syllabic words with lexical stress on the second or third syllable.

Given that lexical and rhythmic stress are both expressed in terms of increased duration in Ukrainian, the existence of pretonic lengthening, which is yet another kind of temporal adjustment in that language, poses an additional descriptive and theoretical challenge. From the descriptive point of view, little is known about the scope of this effect and how it depends on the distance between the beginning of the word and the lexical stress position; another question is that of how duration enhancement interacts with vowel quality (phonetic reduction) in pretonic positions. On the theoretical side, Łukaszewicz and Mołczanow (2018b) suggest that the lexical stress domain extends beyond the lexically stressed syllable in Ukrainian, which may hinder the expression of the alternating rhythmic pattern in the vicinity to the left of lexical stress. If pretonic lengthening is a lexical domain effect, it needs to be clarified how it can interact with rhythmic constraints such as LAPSE-AT-PEAK. It also seems necessary to place the Ukrainian pattern within a broader context of pretonic lengthening effects occurring in other languages, especially those belonging to the East Slavic group.

A subtle increase in vowel duration in the pretonic relative to the pre-pretonic position, similar to the one reported for Ukrainian, has been detected in Romance languages such as European Portuguese, Romanian, and Spanish (Chitoran & Hualde 2007), as well as Modern Hebrew (Cohen *et al.* 2018). A more conspicuous pretonic lengthening effect has been reported for Cordoban Spanish (Lang-Rigal 2014; Lenardón 2017) as well as some East Slavic dialects (Bethin 2006); in both, the pretonic syllable can exceed the lexically stressed syllable in length. Pretonic lengthening may represent a gradient phonetic effect – for example, the strength of this effect may decrease with distance from the lexically stressed vowel (see Cohen *et al.* 2018: 12). In some languages, the extra duration present in the pretonic position has been reported to cause emergence of certain phonological patterns; compare the phonologisation of *iV* sequences in Spanish as diphthongs or hiatus (Chitoran & Hualde 2007: 59).

Pretonic lengthening has been widely documented in East Slavic. In Standard Russian, 'a vowel in a pretonic syllable is longer than a vowel in an unaccented syllable by a quarter to almost half (1.25 to 1.4 approx.)' (Jones 1923/69: 216). This difference has been corroborated by instrumental data reported in Vysotskij (1973: 38), with a 22 ms difference in vocalic duration detected between the first and the second pretonic positions. In East Slavic dialects reported in Vysotskij (1973), there seems to be a special connection between the duration of the immediately pretonic vowel and that of the lexically stressed (tonic) vowel. Correlation analyses conducted on the basis of Vysotskij's data corroborate the observation that the pretonic and tonic syllables constitute a close-knit unit across East Slavic dialects (r (13) = 0.841, p < 0.001), while a rather loose relationship (no significant correlation) is observed between pre-pretonic and pretonic or pre-pretonic and tonic vowels (Łukaszewicz *et al.* submitted). Pretonic lengthening is important from the point of view of the degree of vowel reduction, which is a phonological process in Standard Russian. As we show in Section 2.2.5, Ukrainian is different from Standard Russian not only in terms of temporal patterns (Łukaszewicz & Mołczanow 2018b: 381), but also in terms of how duration adjustments correspond to vowel quality (formant undershoot).

Notably, no similar effect has been reported for the immediately posttonic positions in East Slavic. In this Element, we widen the focus to include both the pretonic and the posttonic positions, supplementing the description by new empirical data from Ukrainian. Posttonic lengthening has not been previously reported for Ukrainian, and its absence, confirmed by the current findings, points to an asymmetrical temporal pattern in syllables located next to lexical stress. A preliminary study based on intrinsic comparisons in three-syllable words having the structure [ˈσσˌσ] and the same vowel category in the posttonic versus final positions – compare /a/ in [ˈʋɨpaˌla] 'fall out, 3rd pers. sg. fem. past ' – demonstrates that the vowel in the posttonic (metrically weak) syllable is conspicuously shorter than the same vowel in the final (metrically strong) syllable; see Figure 6 (Łukaszewicz & Mołczanow 2024). The lengthening of the final syllable cannot simply be a boundary effect in Ukrainian – as illustrated in Section 2.2.4, stress-induced differences are found in extrinsic comparisons of the final syllable in minimal pairs having the structure [ˌσσˈσσ]/[σˈσσˌσ].

We return to pretonic lengthening in Section 3, in which we argue that the scope of this effect is important from the point of view of interaction between the lexical and grammatical stress domains. Specifically, we suggest that lexical stress domain extends leftwards to up to three preceding syllables. As this

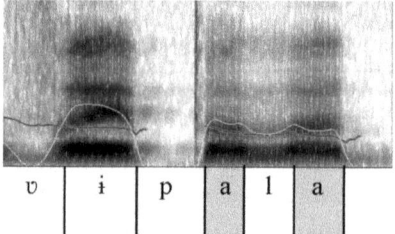

['ʋipa̩ la] 'fall out, 3rd pers. sg. fem. past'

Figure 6 Durational enhancement of the final (metrically strong) vowel relative to the posttonic position.

extension is realised in terms of a gradual increase in duration, pretonic lengthening interferes with the duration-based expression of rhythmic stress (see Section 3.2 for further discussion).

In Section 2.2.4, we consider the confounding effect of word boundaries on the temporal expression of metrical prominence. Specifically, we ask whether the increase in duration observed in initial and final positions in Ukrainian cues rhythmic stress or signals word edges.

2.2.4 Word Boundary Effects

The experiments involving words of five or more syllables have revealed that both primary and secondary stress are cued by increased duration (Łukaszewicz & Mołczanow 2018a, 2018b, 2018c). Duration is a cross-linguistically common correlate of metrical prominence, but it is also a well-known multipurpose phonetic cue. Factors such as word length, segmental structure, phrasal stress, or boundary effects can be confounding factors as far as the expression of word-level prominence is concerned (see e.g. Turk & Shattuck-Hufnagel 2000, 2007; Plag *et al.* 2011; White & Turk 2010; Vogel *et al.* 2016). Furthermore, observed duration adjustments can manifest multiple mechanisms operating simultaneously. An illustrative example is provided by lengthening patterns in English phrases such as *tuna#choir* versus *tune#acquire*. The word-final [ə] in *tuna#choir* is longer than the word-initial [ə] in the segmentally identical phrase *tune#acquire*, whereas the [uː] of the syllable *tun* is longer in the latter example. These temporal patterns can be caused by word-final lengthening (Beckman & Edwards 1990) and other mechanisms, such as asymmetric polysyllabic shortening (Lindblom & Rapp 1972) and syllable ratio equalisation (Abercrombie 1965/71); see Turk and Shattuck-Hufnagel (2000: 401) for further discussion.

As discussed previously, Ukrainian has rhythmic stress which is located, depending on the word length, at both or one of the word edges, and is expressed by prolonged vowel duration. However, given that speakers use duration adjustment mechanisms for multiple prosodic purposes, a question arises whether the increased duration at word edges in Ukrainian cues prosodic prominence or signals word boundaries.

To answer this question, Mołczanow *et al.* (2018, 2021) investigated segmentally identical word pairs differing only in the position of lexical stress and rhythmic structure – for example, [pɔˈpadaˌtɨ] 'fall, inf. perf.' – [ˌpɔpaˈdatɨ] 'strike and hit the mark, inf. imperf.' (cf. 7a). This design made it possible to empirically distinguish between the effects of metrical prominence and lengthening at the word edges, simultaneously controlling for the potential confounding influence of polysyllabic shortening and intrinsic segmental length. The following extrinsic comparisons were performed (7b):

(7) a. $\sigma_1 \, '\sigma_2 \, \sigma_3 \, ,\sigma_4$ e.g. [pɔˈʊodɨˌtɨ] 'behave, inf.'

   $,\sigma_1 \, \sigma_2 \, '\sigma_3 \, \sigma_4$ [ˌpɔʊɔˈdɨtɨ] 'lead, inf. perf.'

b. σ_1: pretonic – secondary   [pɔ] – [ˌpɔ]
   σ_2: tonic – pretonic   [ˈʊɔ] – [ʊɔ]
   σ_3: unstressed – tonic   [dɨ] – [ˈdɨ]
   σ_4: secondary – unstressed   [ˌtɨ] – [tɨ]

The use of segmentally identical minimal pairs ensured that any observed temporal differences reflected differences in prosodic prominence. Fourteen speakers were audio-recorded reading test words which were placed in the frame [skaˈʒɨ ... ˈdrufiij ˈraz] 'Say (2nd pers. sg. imp.) ... for the second time.' The statistical analysis was based on the duration measurements of seven minimal pairs (4,128 vowels and consonants in total).

Overall, the results point to the existence of edge-based prominence independent of boundary strengthening. As illustrated in Figure 7, the word-final [ɨ] is visibly shorter in the metrically weak position in [ˌpɔʊɔˈdɨtɨ] 'lead, inf. perf.' (a) than in the metrically strong position in [pɔˈʊodɨˌtɨ] 'behave, inf.' (b). Additionally, the intrinsic

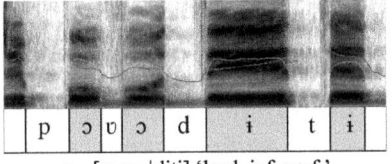
a. [ˌpɔʊɔˈdɨtɨ] 'lead, inf. perf.'

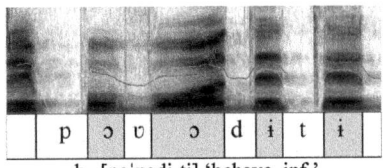
b. [pɔˈʊodɨˌtɨ] 'behave, inf.'

Figure 7 Durational enhancement of the final metrically strong vowel (right panel) relative to the final metrically weak vowel (left panel).

comparison of the posttonic (metrically weak) and final (metrically strong) [ɨ] in [pɔˈʊɔdɨˌtɨ] 'behave, inf.' (right panel) points to increased duration in the latter. The pattern is statistically robust (Łukaszewicz & Mołczanow 2024).

As for the initial position, the measurements revealed the effect of pretonic lengthening. In Figure 7, the pretonic [ɔ] is visibly longer than the rhythmically stressed [ɔ], in the case of the intrinsic comparison of the two vowels in [ˌpɔʊɔˈdɨtɨ] 'lead, inf. perf.' (panel (a)) as well as the extrinsic comparison of the vowel [ɔ] in the initial syllables of [ˌpɔʊɔˈdɨtɨ] 'lead, inf. perf.' (the rhythmic stress condition; panel (a)) and [pɔˈʊɔdɨˌtɨ] 'behave, inf.' (the pretonic condition; panel (b)). Duration measurements conducted for the whole data set revealed a small but statistically significant difference of 7.5 ms between the vowel in the rhythmically weak pretonic position and the vowel in the rhythmically stressed position.

In sum, the comparison of temporal patterns in segmentally identical syllables indicates that word-final rhythmic stress and pretonic lengthening are separate duration-based mechanisms independent of temporal adjustments associated with word boundaries. As we will see in Section 2.3.1, this result is confirmed by extrinsic comparisons of identical syllables in trisyllabic words.

2.2.5 Vowel Reduction

This section presents the results of our previous research on the relation between duration and vowel quality vis-à-vis the metrical structure in Ukrainian. It is well known that duration may interact with vowel formants to signal metrical prominence. As word stress is inextricably related to the phenomenon of vowel reduction, a comprehensive account of a prosodic system cannot dispense with the study of the effect of metrical prominence on the expression of vocalic contrasts. Vowel reduction can be categorical (i.e. leading to a loss of lexical contrast) or phonetic, typically resulting in non-categorical (gradient) shrinkage of the vocalic space. Ukrainian does not have phonological reduction, unlike, for example, typologically close Belarusian, which displays categorical neutralisation of lexical distinctions in unstressed positions (Toc'ka 1969; Czekman and Smułkowa 1988). This is illustrated by the alternation [o] – [a] in Belarusian in (8a) and its absence in Ukrainian in (8b):

(8) a. [ˈkɔzɨ]   –   [kaˈza]   *Belarusian*
    b. [ˈkɔzɨ]   –   [kɔˈza]   *Ukrainian*
    'she-goat, nom. pl.' 'id., nom. sg.'

Phonetic reduction, in turn, is widely attested in unstressed positions in a variety of languages and may either accompany phonological reduction or occur in its absence. Phonetic reduction usually consists in the reduction in duration, spectral reduction, or both. This type of reduction has been reported for many languages – for example, Swedish (Lindblom 1963), Dutch (Beinum & Jeannette 1980), English (Moon & Lindblom 1994), and Polish (Nowak 2006, Strycharczuk *et al.* 2021).

Phonetic vowel reduction has been standardly described in terms of gestural undershoot attributed to decreased duration in prosodically weak contexts (Lindblom 1963; Flemming 2004; Barnes 2006). In the classical vowel reduction model of Lindblom (1963), the first vowel formant (F1) is shown to be a function of the decreasing vowel duration in unstressed vowels in Swedish. Subsequent studies have found that the compression of vowel space can also be caused by shorter segment durations associated with faster speaking rates (e.g. Miller 1981; Flege 1988; Agwuele *et al.* 2008, among many others). Interestingly, other studies have shown that the effect of temporal reduction on vowel quality is not automatic, in that reduced duration can be dissociated from formant undershoot on a language-specific basis (Delattre 1965; Fourakis 1991; Beckman *et al.* 1992; Barnes 2006; Nadeu 2014, and others). For instance, Barnes (2006) reveals a strong correlation between F1 and duration in the second pretonic but not in the pretonic position in Russian. Barnes (2006) interprets this finding – that is, duration-dependent reduction in the second pretonic position versus duration-independent reduction in the pretonic position – in terms of structural differences: reduction in the first pretonic position is categorical (phonological), whereas reduction in the second pretonic position is gradient (phonetic).

Vowel neutralisations in Ukrainian are non-categorical and consist in centralisation and vowel undershoot (Toc'ka 1973: 186; Mołczanow *et al.* 2019b; Łukaszewicz *et al.* submitted). An experimental study by Toc'ka (1973) indicates that vowel quality may play a role in expressing secondary stress. Based on data collected from five speakers coming from central Ukraine, Toc'ka (1973) reports that the distinctive vowel quality is maintained in some unstressed positions. Specifically, the measures of formant values of unstressed vowels show that qualitative reduction is suspended in positions removed by one or two syllables from the main stress. Toc'ka (1973) finds qualitative differences in unstressed positions only for the vowels [a], [u], and [ɛ], and she does not relate the presence of vocalic undershoot to any rhythmic pattern. The presence of phonetic vowel reduction has been detected in more recent acoustic studies (Mołczanow *et al.* 2019b; Łukaszewicz *et al.* submitted) which conducted formant measurements of the vowel [a] in all positions preceding lexical stress.[6] The analysis of acoustic data reveals subtle lengthening of the

---

[6] Our research on vowel reduction has been limited to the investigation of the vowel [a] due to the exploratory nature of these experiments, whose main goal has been to find out whether there exist differences in the formant structure of rhythmically stressed and rhythmically unstressed

pretonic vowel and formant undershoot across the lexically unstressed syllables. Interestingly, these findings indicate that the relationship between temporal and spectral parameters is not the same in the metrically strong and weak positions.

The measurements of the formant structure of the vowel [a] were conducted based on pentasyllabic (and quadrisyllabic) words with lexical stress falling on the fourth syllable – that is, words having the structure [,$\sigma_1\sigma_2\sigma_3$'$\sigma_4(\sigma_5)$]. While a small progressive increase in vowel duration was observed across the three positions preceding lexical stress, only the pretonic position (σ_3) was significantly different, and the initial (σ_1) and second (σ_2) positions were comparable in length. Interestingly, a significant positive correlation between F1 and duration was detected for the second unstressed vowel (σ_2) (r(291) = 0.19) and the pretonic vowel (σ_3) (r(286) = 0.46) but not for the initial (rhythmic) vowel (r(289) = $-$ 0.075); see Figure 8). Similarly to the initial (rhythmic) position, vowels in the lexically stressed (tonic) positions (σ_4) did not display a correlation between F1 and duration. We have tentatively concluded that this stability of F1 targets in metrically strong positions (i.e. the positions of rhythmic and lexical stress) might serve as another cue to metrical prominence (Mołczanow *et al.* 2019b; Łukaszewicz *et al.* submitted). Alternatively, as we point out in Łukaszewicz *et al.* (submitted), duration-independent stable F1 targets may also point to phonologisation of vowel reduction in the initial position.

We return to the issue of vowel reduction in Section 2.3.3, where we present new data drawn from duration and format measurements of vowels in shorter (trisyllabic) words. These new findings show that the relationship between F1 and duration is more complex than suggested by the results of previous studies discussed in this section and may also depend on such factors as word length or the relative position of lexical stress with respect to the word's left versus right edge.

2.2.6 Interim Summary

In sum, previous research on Ukrainian points to a rather complex relationship between metrical phonology and phonetics, with some non-obvious surface-level effects resulting from the interaction of various prosodic factors manifested in

---

positions. However, let us note that there are reports in the literature that mid vowels undergo raising when followed by high vowels in the following syllable, which is subject to much dialectal variation (see Toc'ka 1970, 1973 and Zales'kyj 1973 for further discussion). To the best of our knowledge, these reduction patterns have not been systematically investigated with the use of the up-to-date methodology.

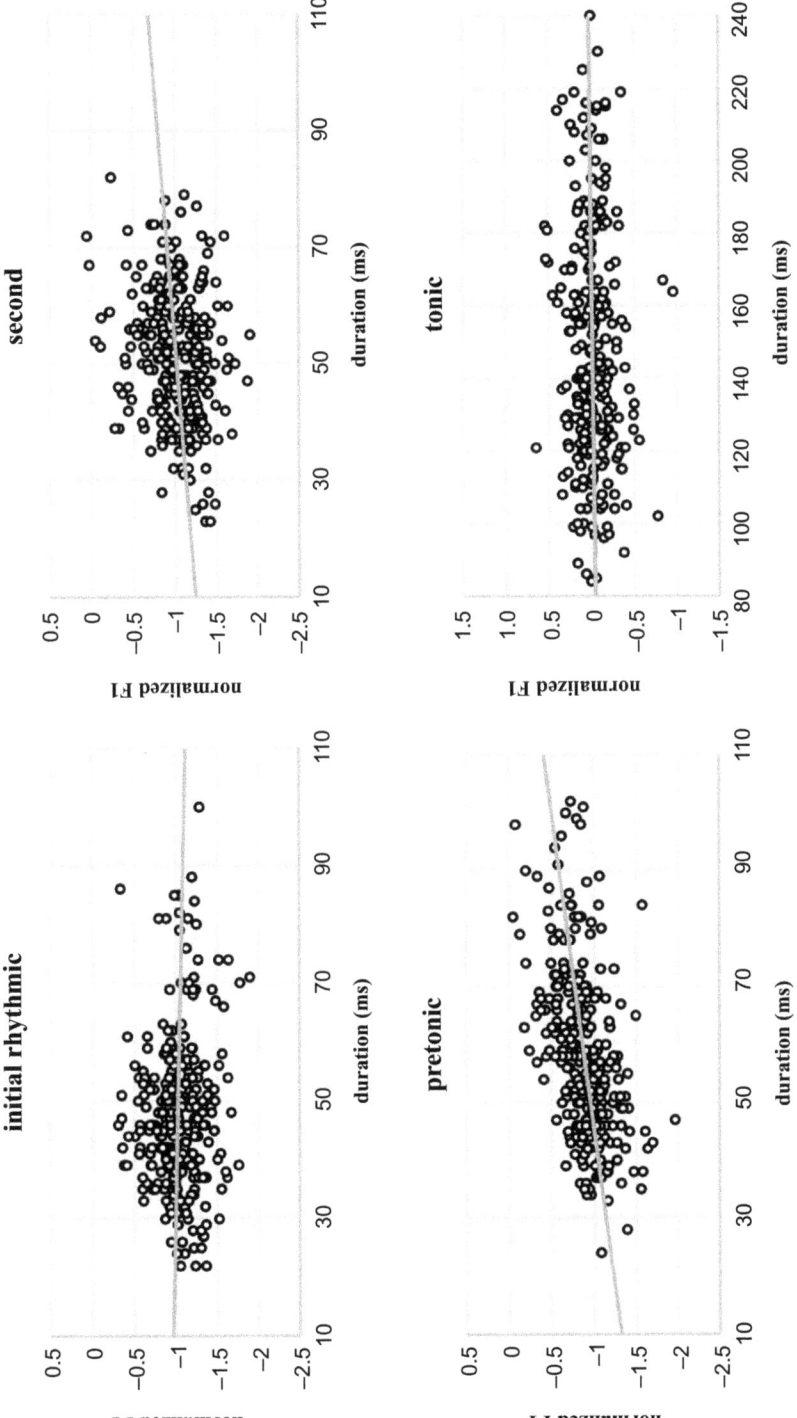

Figure 8 The relationship between normalised F1 and duration in [ˌσσσˈσ(σ)] words, divided by position.

terms of temporal enhancement. Acoustic measurements in polysyllabic words, such as those in Figure 4 and Figure 5, suggest some interesting asymmetry on the phonetic level: the syllables immediately to the left of the lexically stressed position show a subtle lengthening effect, while those to the right do not. In Section 2.3, we look at temporal patterns in three-syllable words in Ukrainian. The point of interest is whether three-syllable words having the 'mirror-image' metrical structures, [ˈσσˌσ] versus [ˌσσˈσ], exhibit a degree of (a)symmetry in the leftward versus rightward pattern on the phonetic level, comparable to that occurring in the 'mirror-image' six-syllable words, [ˈσσσˌσσˌσ] and [ˌσσˌσσσˈσ]. Does the pretonic position differ significantly from the posttonic one in such short words? Moreover, considering the relatively small two-syllable distance between the word's beginning and lexical stress in words having the structure [ˌσσˈσ], we expect either the predicted rightward rhythmic pattern or pretonic lengthening to occur, but not both. Do then the temporal patterns across the first two syllables in [ˌσσˈσ] words resemble the initial rhythmic [ˌσσ-] pattern of [ˌσσˌσσσˈσ] words, or rather show the gradual 'pretonic lengthening' effect in the vicinity of lexical stress? Which of the two competing phenomena, rhythmic stress or pretonic lengthening, prevails in such words? We also tackle the question of the relationship between duration and formant structure in different prosodic positions in those words.

2.3 Experiment: Three-Syllable Words

We discuss here the results of an acoustic study in which we conducted duration measurements in three-syllable words with lexical stress on the first, second, and third syllables: [ˈσσˌσ], [σˈσσ], and [ˌσσˈσ]. Three-syllable words are convenient to focus on as their compact structure allows us to immediately grasp the dependencies among the three word positions and the varying stress conditions related to the placement of lexical stress.

The measured segment was the vowel [a], which appeared in segmentally identical sequences, *pad, kat, sad, zad*, across the three word positions, initial – medial – final, and across different stress conditions. In total, nine conditions result in which a given sequence can be found, reflecting different combinations of stress and position, listed in (9). The examples in (9) all contain the sequence *pad*, which was one of the four sequences used. The flanking consonants *p_d* are both followed by vowels. In the case of the final position, in which the vowel [a] occurs in an open syllable, as in [ˈt͡ʃɛrɛˌpa] 'skull, gen. sg.', the *d* marks the onset of the following part of the frame, which began with the word [ˈdrufiɪj] 'second' (see Section 2.3.1). Such segmental comparability is essential because, as we discuss later, this set of data was also used for formant measurement in vowels.

(9) a. word-initial lexical stress
    ˈσ σ ˌσ [ˈpadaˌti] 'fall, inf.'   lexical stress (initial)
    ˈσ σ ˌσ [ˈnapaˌdi] 'attack, nom. pl.'   posttonic (medial)
    ˈσ σ ˌσ [ˈt͡ʃɛrɛˌpa] 'skull, gen. sg.'   rhythmic (final)

  b. word-medial lexical stress
    σ ˈσ σ [paˈdut͡ʃa] 'falling, nom. sg.'   pretonic (initial)
    σ ˈσ σ [pɔˈpadaʊ] 'fall, masc. sg. perf. past' lexical stress (medial)
    σ ˈσ σ [kaˈnapa] 'sofa, nom. sg.'   post-tonic (final)

  c. word-final lexical stress
    ˌσ σ ˈσ [ˌpadɛˈʒʲi] 'cattle sickness, nom. pl.' rhythmic (initial)
    ˌσ σ ˈσ [ˌnapaˈdaj] 'attack, imp.'   pretonic (medial)
    ˌσ σ ˈσ [ˌlistɔˈpad] 'November, nom. sg.'   lexical stress (final)

There are five stress conditions resulting from the metrical structure of three-syllable words – initial rhythmic, pretonic, lexical stress (tonic), posttonic, and final rhythmic.[7] These conditions are not represented equally across the word's syllables – only lexical stress occurs in three word positions (initial/medial/final), whereas pretonic and posttonic positions are represented twice (pretonic: initial/medial, posttonic: medial/final), and initial and final rhythmic stress occur in one position, initial and final respectively. Since all three word positions can bear lexical stress, this gives us an opportunity to test whether there is a purely positional effect on the expression of lexical stress based on the duration parameter. In turn, both pretonic and posttonic conditions occur in the second syllable in [ˌσ σ ˈσ] vs. [ˈσ σ ˌσ] words, which makes it possible to compare them directly, avoiding a potential positional confound. The rhythmic condition is limited to the initial and final positions, where it can be juxtaposed directly against pretonic versus posttonic conditions respectively. Because our primary interest is the potential asymmetry between the leftward and rightward pattern, in our statistical analyses that follow, we refer to the initial and final rhythmic stress conditions separately, rather than collapsing them into a single category.

The structure of three-syllable words allows us to consider the role of several potentially important factors on the basis of a single data set:

(i) anticipatory effect of lexical stress (pretonic lengthening)
(ii) preservatory effect of lexical stress (posttonic lengthening)
(iii) initial/final rhythmicity
(iv) initial/final ('boundary') effects independent of stress
(v) general positional effects

---

[7] As mentioned earlier, there has been a time-honoured tradition to refer to the lexical stress position as 'tonic' in Slavic linguistics. We refer to the unstressed conditions as 'pretonic' or 'posttonic', depending on whether they precede or follow the lexically stressed syllable.

2.3.1 Methods

Ten native speakers of Ukrainian (9F, 1M; aged $M = 48$) took part in the experiment. To minimise dialectal variation, we selected participants who came from western Ukraine (Lviv, Lutsk, Ivano-Frankivsk, and Rivne regions). Seven participants were recorded in Ukraine and three in Warsaw in Poland. The participants recorded in Ukraine were monolingual; the participants recorded in Poland reported some knowledge of Polish but used Ukrainian in everyday speech.

The recordings were performed using a Tascam Dr-100mkIII portable recorder, set at a sampling rate of 44.1 kHz, and an AT897 microphone. Participants were audio-recorded reading sentences containing target words in three repetitions. The words put in a frame were presented on a computer monitor; the list was randomised to avoid order effects. Apart from target items, twenty filler words were used. Lexical stress was marked orthographically to facilitate the identification of words. We obtained 1,080 tokens in total (10 participants * 9 stress/position conditions * 4 segmental types * 3 repetitions). Target words all appeared in the same frame: [ˈskaʒɛˌtɛ ... ˈdrufiij ˈraz] 'You (pl.) will say ... for the second time'. Twenty-one tokens (1.9% of data) were rejected during analysis because of speech dysfluencies.

Segmentation was done manually using a high-resolution waveform editor (*Sound Forge Pro* v. 11.0); vowel boundaries were marked based on the dynamics of changes in the shape of the waveform, the visual inspection of the spectrogram in *Praat*, and auditory perception. Measurements were conducted in *Praat* (v. 6.2.09; Boersma & Weenink 2022); duration values were obtained using a script. Raw duration values, expressed in [ms], were used to calculate by speaker z-scores in order to make the data more comparable.

2.3.2 Temporal Patterns

We performed two kinds of statistical analysis: (i) an overall analysis testing the effect of stress on duration across all tokens, and (ii) planned comparisons targeting selected prosodic and positional effects which could be tested on the basis of subsets of data. For statistical analyses, we used linear mixed effects models, built in SPSS (v. 29).

The overall analysis included standardised duration (z-scores) as the dependent variable and 'stress' as well as 'trial' as fixed effects. The 'stress' condition had five levels: initial rhythmic, pretonic, lexical (tonic), posttonic, and final rhythmic; the trial effect had three levels (corresponding to the number of repetitions in the experiment). To account for the repeated measures (identical segmental contexts) occurring in the experiment, we added 'sequence' as a random effect – the model included the sequence-specific intercept and slope for the fixed effect of stress. Individual differences in speech rates were controlled in terms of by-speaker z-scores; however, there still might be individual differences related to the expression of stress. To control for such effects, we included by-speaker random slopes for the fixed effect of stress in our model.

Significant results were obtained for both 'stress' and 'trial' conditions. The model had a marginal R^2 of 0.86 (reflecting the proportion of variance explained by fixed factors alone), and a conditional R^2 of 0.88 (reflecting the proportion of variance explained by both fixed and random factors). The estimated means for particular stress conditions are depicted in Figure 9. The final rhythmic syllable, which was the reference level in the analysis, turned out significantly different from all other 'stress' positions, except the pretonic one; initial rhythmic: $\beta_1 = -0.206$, $SE = 0.056$, $t = -3.715$, $p < 0.001$; pretonic: $\beta_2 = -0.068$, $SE = 0.051$, $t = -1.347$, $p = 0.188$; lexical: $\beta_3 = 1.826$, $SE = 0.049$, $t = 37.166$, $p < 0.001$; posttonic: $\beta_4 = -0.205$, $SE = 0.051$, $t = -4.041$, $p < 0.001$. As anticipated, the most conspicuous temporal enhancement was found in the lexical stress position. Also, the 'final rhythmic' vowel turns out significantly longer than the 'posttonic' vowel in this analysis. This is an important result because it corroborates the presence of rhythmic stress in Ukrainian. A similar effect of final rhythmic stress was reported in Mołczanow et al. (2018). Additional paired comparisons reveal a significant, but very small difference of 0.138 (z-scores), $p < 0.05$, between the pretonic vowel and the one in the initial rhythmic condition, pointing to a subtle pretonic lengthening effect. In

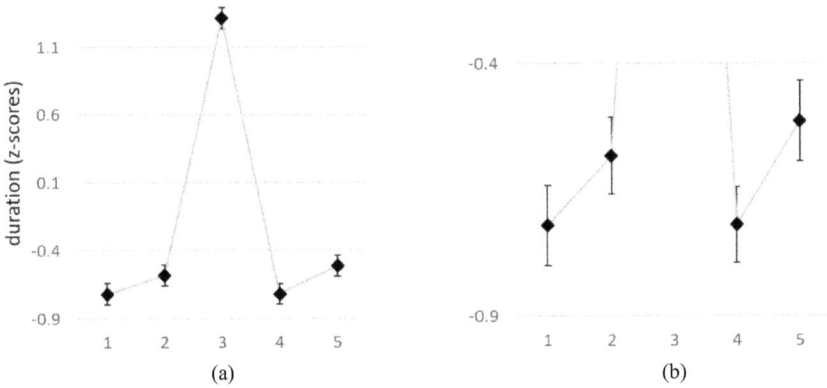

Figure 9 (a) Duration (z-scores) across the five stress conditions: 1 – initial rhythmic, 2 – pretonic, 3 – lexical stress, 4 – posttonic, 5 – final rhythmic; (b) the enlarged fragment.

addition, a comparison between the pretonic and posttonic conditions reveals that the pretonic vowel is longer than the posttonic one; the difference is small (0.137 z-duration), but statistically significant ($p < 0.01$). This suggests a rightward–leftward asymmetry in temporal patterns, similar to the one occurring in the vicinity of lexical stress in longer words (recall the discussion in Section 2.3.1).

Regarding the trial effect, the third trial was shorter than the first one; $\beta = 0.086$, $SE = 0.026$, $t = 3.263$, $p < 0.001$. The effect was significant but, again, very small.

As we can see in Figure 9, the resultant pattern across the syllables preceding the lexically stressed position is clearly not a mirror image of the pattern occurring across the syllables following lexical stress. It seems, then, that in three-syllable words, the leftward alternating rhythm – that is, the one propagating from the end of the word – appears as predicted by the metrical theory. However, the rightward one (i.e. the one propagating from the beginning of the word) is not reified in such words, as pretonic lengthening supersedes it.

We also conducted four additional analyses to test whether

- any positional effects exist independently of stress,
- whether the pretonic and posttonic conditions are significantly different from each other independently of the word position,
- whether pretonic versus initial rhythmic conditions, as well as posttonic versus final rhythmic conditions are significantly different independently of position.

For the purpose of the first analysis, we used a subset of data containing only lexically stressed vowels. We tested the effect of position, initial (the first syllable in the word), medial (the second syllable in the word), final (the third syllable in the word), while keeping the stress condition constant. The linear mixed effects model included 'position' and 'trial' as the fixed effects; the random structure was analogous to the one in our general model, the only difference being that the random slopes were used for the fixed effect of 'position', not for the fixed effect of 'stress'. We obtained a significant effect of 'trial', but not that of 'position'. The third syllable is slightly longer than the first one, the difference being close to the threshold of significance: $\beta = -0.285$, $SE = 0.1$, $t = -2.108$ ($p = 0.05$). The statistical results thus point to a potential gradual and subtle lengthening effect across the entire word.

In the second analysis, we compared the pretonic and posttonic conditions in exactly the same position within the word, which was the medial (second) syllable; compare [ˈσ σ ˌσ] (posttonic) and [ˌσ σ ˈσ] (pretonic). (Because of convergence problems we had to remove the sequence-specific slopes in this analysis.) Of particular interest to us here is whether the pretonic and posttonic conditions remain significantly different from each other when the word position is kept constant. This expectation is borne out. The pretonic condition turns out significantly different from the posttonic condition, which is the reference category in our linear mixed effects analysis: $\beta = 0.224$, $SE = 0.05$, $t = 4.394$, $p < 0.001$. We conclude that the pretonic vowel is longer than the posttonic one. There was no significant effect of trial in that analysis.

Finally, we test whether rhythmic stress exists as a significant effect independently of the initial/final position. This is an important question because in three-syllable words, rhythmic stress can appear only at word edges; thus, hypothetically, it could simply be a boundary strengthening effect unconnected with stress. We conducted two separate analyses for the initial and final syllables, containing the relevant stress conditions. In both analyses, the models converged with the fully specified random structure. We did not obtain a significant result for the difference between the initial rhythmic condition and the pretonic condition within the subset of data limited to the first syllable in the word ($p = 0.085$). However, the analysis of potential stress effects in the third syllable yielded significant results. The posttonic (unstressed) condition turns out significantly shorter from the final rhythmic condition, which is the reference category ($\beta = -0.157$, $SE = 0.051$, $t = -3.106$, $p < 0.05$).

To wind up, both the overall analysis as well as additional detailed statistical analyses point to phonetic asymmetry in durational patterns in three-syllable words. It is noteworthy that the present measurements are in principle consistent with the description of Toc'ka (1973: 172), who reports the following relative vowel durations in three-syllable words (vowel length has been represented on a scale from 0.75 to 2, where 2 stands for maximal duration of stressed vowels): 2 – 1 – 1.75, 1 – 2 – 1.5, 0.75 – 1 – 2. Similarly to the results obtained in the current study, this description reveals an asymmetric temporal pattern in [ˌσ σ 'σ] vs. ['σ σ ˌσ] words, with a duration increase in final rhythmically stressed syllables (2 – 1 – 1.75) and a gradual increase in duration across pretonic syllables in words with rhythmic stress on the initial syllable (0.75 – 1 – 2). These duration patterns show that the words which are expected to be mirror images of each other from the point of view of metrical theory – compare [ˌσ σ 'σ] and ['σ σ ˌσ] – are not symmetrical on the phonetic level. While the final rhythmic prominence is seen in ['σ σ ˌσ] words, no initial rhythmic prominence is found in [ˌσ σ 'σ] words. Instead, it is a gradual lengthening effect across the syllables preceding lexical stress that prevails in such words. This agrees with the pretonic lengthening pattern reported earlier for longer words, in which the otherwise regular alternation of rhythmic beats was found to disappear in the vicinity of lexical stress (Łukaszewicz & Mołczanow 2018b). If, as suggested in previous work (Łukaszewicz & Mołczanow 2018b; Łukaszewicz et al. submitted), pretonic lengthening is viewed as the lexical stress domain extension, the Ukrainian data can shed light on the interaction between lexical and grammatical stress domains, and the extent of application of rhythmic stress.

2.3.3 Vowel Reduction (F1 Undershoot)

The relationship between duration and vowel quality vis-à-vis the metrical structure in Ukrainian has been tested thus far only on the basis of [ˌσσσ'σ (σ)] words (as presented in Section 2.2.5). As the scope of previous studies (Mołczanow et al. 2019b; Łukaszewicz et al. submitted) was limited to metrical positions occurring to the left of lexical stress, little is known about formant undershoot in posttonic positions and its relation to metrical structure in Ukrainian. Here we present novel data on F1/duration patterns in three-syllable words, using the same data set which was analysed in Section 2.3.2. The measured segment is the vowel [a] occurring in nine different stress/position conditions, as schematised and illustrated earlier in (9).

To test for the presence of vowel undershoot, we measured F1 in the vowel [a] using the Burg LPC algorithm in *Praat* (v. 6.2.09; Boersma & Weenink 2022). Measurements were conducted at acoustic midpoints using a *Praat* script, with the ceiling of the formant search range being 5,000 Hz for male speakers and 5,500 Hz for female speakers. The data were balanced with respect to the places of articulation of the flanking consonants, which allowed us to minimise the effect of asymmetrical consonantal contexts. In order to ensure data comparability across speakers, formant frequencies in [Hz] were converted to a normalised acoustic space by calculating by speaker z-scores (cf. Lobanov 1971).

Two kinds of statistical analyses in terms of linear mixed effects models were performed. The first set of analyses was designed to test whether there would be a significant effect of stress on F1. As F1 correlates negatively with vowel height, we expect the vowel [a] to show lower F1 in metrically weak positions relative to metrically strong positions; lack of reduction is expected especially in the lexical stress position (Mołczanow et al. 2019b; Łukaszewicz et al. submitted). The second set of analyses was implemented to examine the relationship between two continuous parameters, F1 and duration, depending on stress and position. The point of interest here is whether the stress-induced duration decrease in Ukrainian goes hand in hand with an automatic reduction in vowel quality (F1 undershoot). A preliminary analysis over the aggregated data from all nine stress/position conditions points to a strong positive correlation between F1 and duration; $r(1,059) = 0.8$, $p < 0.001$. Because the relationship between F1 and duration is clearly non-linear (as demonstrated in Figure 10,

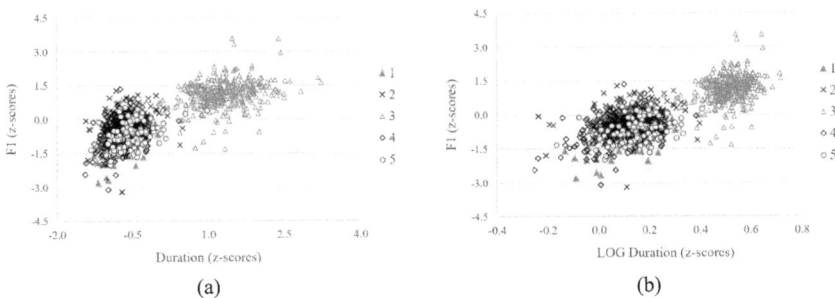

Figure 10 F1 (z-scores) versus duration (z-scores) – (a) raw and (b) log, depending on the stress condition: 1 – initial rhythmic, 2 – pretonic, 3 – lexical stress, 4 – posttonic, 5 – final rhythmic.

panel (a)), in this analysis the duration values were transformed using a logarithm (a constant was first added to ensure that all duration z-scores would end up above zero). The result of this transformation is visible in panel (b). This preliminary analysis does not inform us whether there is an independent effect of stress on F1 after the effect of duration has been accounted for, which is the problem we address in the second set of analyses.

In the first set of analyses, we built a linear mixed effects model with F1 as the dependent variable, and 'stress' and 'trial' as fixed factors. Analogously to the model described in Section 2.3.2, the 'stress' condition had five levels (initial rhythmic, pretonic, lexical (tonic), posttonic, final rhythmic); the trial effect had three levels (reflecting the number of repetitions in the experiment). To account for the repeated measures (identical segmental contexts) occurring in the experiment, we added 'sequence' as a random effect – the model included sequence-specific intercepts and slopes for the fixed effect of 'stress'. Individual differences in F1 were controlled in terms of z-scores, which made the random effect of 'speaker' redundant; however, by-speaker random slopes for the fixed effect of 'stress' were included to account for potential differences in the degree of reduction related to stress.

The effect of stress was significant, but that of trial was not. The final rhythmic vowel, which is the reference level in the analysis, turns out to be significantly different only from the lexically stressed vowel ($\beta = 1.735$, $SE = 0.191$, $t = 9.062$, $p < 0.001$). This points to reduced vowel quality across all lexically unstressed positions. As anticipated, in paired comparisons the lexical stress level is significantly different from all other stress levels. The biggest difference in F1 values is found between the lexical stress position and the initial rhythmic stress (1.905, $SE = 0.191$, $p < 0.001$). There is also a statistically significant difference between the initial rhythmically stressed and pretonic vowel (-0.504, $SE = 0.192$, $p < 0.05$). Figure 11 illustrates the estimated

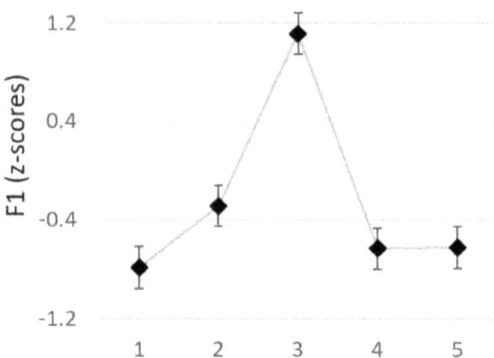

Figure 11 F1 (z-scores) at acoustic midpoints across the five stress conditions: 1 – initial rhythmic, 2 – pretonic, 3 – lexical stress, 4 – posttonic, 5 – final rhythmic.

marginal means for standardised F1 depending on the level of the 'stress' condition.

This model achieves a marginal R^2 of 0.62, which reflects the proportion of the variance for F1 explained by the fixed effect of stress. This proportion is smaller than the proportion of the variance for duration explained in the analogous model in Section 2.3.2, which had a marginal R^2 of 0.86 (the effect of 'trial' is negligible in both models). The linear mixed effects model with duration as the dependent variable wins over the analogous model with F1 as the dependent variable also in terms of −2log likelihood, a goodness-of-fit criterion; it also fares better in terms the Bayesian Information Criterion (BIC), which assesses the trade-off between goodness of fit and the number of parameters used, to prevent the risk of overfitting. In model selection, models with lower −2log likelihood and lower BIC indices are preferred. A comparison of the two models along those two criteria reveals much smaller indices in the duration-based model than in the analogous F1-based model (the duration-based model: −2log likelihood = 800, BIC = 877 vs. the F1-based model: −2log likelihood = 1,698, BIC = 1,775). Next we address the relationship between duration and F1 in more detail.

In order to test whether there is an independent effect of stress on F1 after the effect of duration has been accounted for, we built a baseline model with F1 as the dependent variable, which included the fixed factor of 'trial', duration as well as by-speaker slopes and by-sequence random intercepts and slopes for duration, and then compared it to models augmented in an up-step fashion, first to additionally include (i) the fixed effect of stress as well as by-speaker slopes and by-sequence random intercepts and slopes for stress, and then (ii) also the stress*duration interaction term (cf. Strycharczuk *et al.* 2021). The stress-based models were compared against the baseline model in terms of goodness of fit (likelihood ratios) and variance explained (marginal R^2). There were statistically significant differences between the baseline and stress-based models in terms of the likelihood ratios: $\chi^2(6) = 155.14, p < 0.001$ (baseline vs. model i), $\chi^2(4) = 22.32, p < 0.001$ (model i vs. model ii); also increases in R^2 were detectable: 0.63 (baseline) < 0.66 (model i) < 0.67 (model ii).

Apart from the overall analysis, additional statistical analyses were conducted, focusing on F1 patterns occurring in selected portions of the data set. All initial models included fully specified random effects (by-speaker and by-sequence intercepts and slopes) for the relevant fixed effects (position or stress depending on the analysis); however, not all models converged, in which case the random structure was reduced. We first used a linear mixed effects model to test whether F1 is affected by the position within the word – initial, medial, or final. We used a subset of data containing only lexically stressed vowels. (Recall that lexical stress was the only stress level represented across all three positions within the word.) The third position, which was the reference position in the analysis, turns out to be different from the other two positions at the significance level of $\alpha = 0.05$; compare the difference between the first and the third positions: $\beta = 0.209, SE = 0.075, t = 2.770, p < 0.01$; the difference between the second and the third positions: $\beta = 0.179, SE = 0.076, t = 2.364, p < 0.05$. Comparing this result with the one obtained for duration in Section 2.3.2, we can observe that the vowel in the final syllable is slightly reduced in terms of quality, but not in terms of length, in comparison with vowels in the preceding syllables.

The analyses divided by position additionally reveal some non-automatic relationship between F1 and duration. There is a statistically significant difference in the initial position between the initial rhythmic and pretonic levels, amounting to $\beta = -0.481, SE = 0.085, t = -5.672, p < 0.001$. Thus there is more reduction in the initial rhythmic than pretonic vowel in the first syllable of the word, although no significant difference in duration is reported for exactly the same subset of data. In the second position, the difference between the pretonic and posttonic levels is also significant: $\beta = 0.452, SE = 0.16, t = 2.761, p < 0.05$. This result points to a less reduced quality in the pretonic vowel, which is accompanied by a relatively increased length of that vowel (as revealed by the analysis described in Section 2.3.2). In the third syllable, there is no significant difference in F1 between the posttonic and the final rhythmic position. However, there is a significant difference between those two positions in terms of duration – as the analysis in Section 2.3.2 shows, the final rhythmic vowel is longer.

Synthesising the present and previous results on vowel formant stability vis-à-vis varying duration points to the existence of vowel undershoot in Ukrainian, but also reveals the complexity of that relation, possibly involving such mediating factors as metrical stress, word position, word length, and the distance between lexical stress and edge(s) of the word. Hopefully, this study is a step towards a better understanding of those intricacies, with the non-automatic relationship between F1 and duration to be addressed in more detail in future research.

2.3.4 Other Parameters

Measurements of other parameters which are standardly associated with prominence – that is, pitch and intensity – were also conducted (e.g. Lehiste 1970). A *Praat* script was used to extract peak intensity (Intensity_max), peak F0 (F0_max), and F0 slope. To reflect the well-known non-linearity of human perception, in the case of intensity and pitch, measurements are expressed using a logarithmic rather than linear scale. Intensity was measured in decibels [dB]. F0 was originally measured in Hertz [Hz], with the autocorrelation algorithm and different range settings for male (75–300 Hz) and female speakers (100–500 Hz). Next, the F0 maximum and minimum values were transformed to semitones [ST] relative to the lower limit of the measurement range, using the following formula: $12*(\log_2(F0\_max/min_i/F0\_threshold))$, where $F0\_max/min_i$ is the ith measurement of the F0 maximum (or minimum) and F0_threshold equals 75 Hz for male speakers and 100 Hz for female speakers. Because the differences in perceived prominence may also be related to differences in pitch changes (e.g. rising vs. falling pitch; see Hermes & Rump 1994), F0 slope was calculated in accordance with the standard formula, whereby the difference between the standardised F0 maximum and minimum values is divided by the interval between the time points at which those F0 values were measured: F0_slope = (STF0_max-STF0_min)/(max_time-min_time). Therefore, the F0 slope is measured in semitones per second [ST/s].

Separate statistical analyses were conducted for peak intensity (Intensity_max), peak F0 (F0_max), and F0 slope as dependent variables, using linear mixed effects models. The independent factors in all analyses were the same as in the previous analyses involving duration and F1 – that is, 'stress' and 'trial'. The random effects included speaker- and sequence-specific intercepts and slopes.

In the statistical analysis with intensity as the dependent factor, both 'stress' and 'trial' emerge as significant effects. The final rhythmic position (the reference level in the analysis) is not significantly different from the posttonic position; however, it is significantly different from the lexical stress, pretonic, and initial rhythmic positions; the difference between lexical stress and final rhythmic: $β = 1.718$, $SE = 0.256$, $t = 6.703$, $p < 0.001$; the difference between pretonic and final rhythmic: $β = 1.524$, $SE = 0.271$, $t = 5.63$, $p < 0.001$; the difference between initial rhythmic and final rhythmic: $β = 1.145$, $SE = 0.313$, $t = 3.659$, $p < 0.001$. Paired comparisons across the five 'stress' levels further confirm that the major observed effect is a significant abrupt decline of 1.7 dB between the lexical stress and the posttonic position. There also seems to be a gradual increase in intensity across the first three syllables, with the initial rhythmic position being significantly different from the lexical stress position (−0.5 dB), but not from the pretonic position. The results are presented in Figure 12 (panel (a)).

Analogous statistical analyses were performed for the maximum F0 and the F0 slope. (In the case of the latter parameter, a simpler intercept-only random structure was used.) No significant effect of 'stress' was obtained for the maximum F0; see Figure 12 (panel (b)). For the F0 slope, all estimated marginal means show negative values, pointing to the presence of a falling F0 pattern within a vocalic interval across all five stress levels; see Figure 12 (panel (c)). Relevant from the point of view of metrical prominence marking is the value of F0 slope in the lexical stress position, which is conspicuously different from the values of that parameter in neighbouring positions, pretonic and posttonic. In paired comparisons, there are significant differences between the pretonic and lexical stress positions (−37.133 ST/s, $p < 0.001$) as well as the lexical stress and posttonic positions (29.969 ST/s, $p < 0.001$), but no significant difference between the initial rhythmic and pretonic vowels, nor between the posttonic and final rhythmic vowels. The much flatter slope in the lexical stress position relative to other positions may be due to the longer duration interval in that position, rather than a smaller F0 range. An additional linear mixed effects analysis involving the F0 range (= STF0_max-STF0_min) demonstrates a significantly greater F0 decrease within the lexical stress position ($EM = 3.824$) in comparison with the other positions (initial rhythmic: $EM = 2.382$ ST; pretonic: $EM = 2.543$ ST; posttonic: $EM = 2.385$ ST; final rhythmic: $M = 2.574$ ST; *EMs* stand for 'estimated marginal means'); see Figure 12 (panel (d)). There are no significant effects on F0 parameters connected with initial or final rhythmic stress.

2.4 Summary

This section synthesises the results of the experiment based on trisyllabic words reported in Section 2.3 with our previous studies investigating the acoustic correlates of rhythmic and lexical stress discussed in Section 2.2. Overall, these studies indicate that rhythmic stress is present in Ukrainian and is manifested acoustically by increased vowel duration. However, detailed measurements reveal that the rhythmic

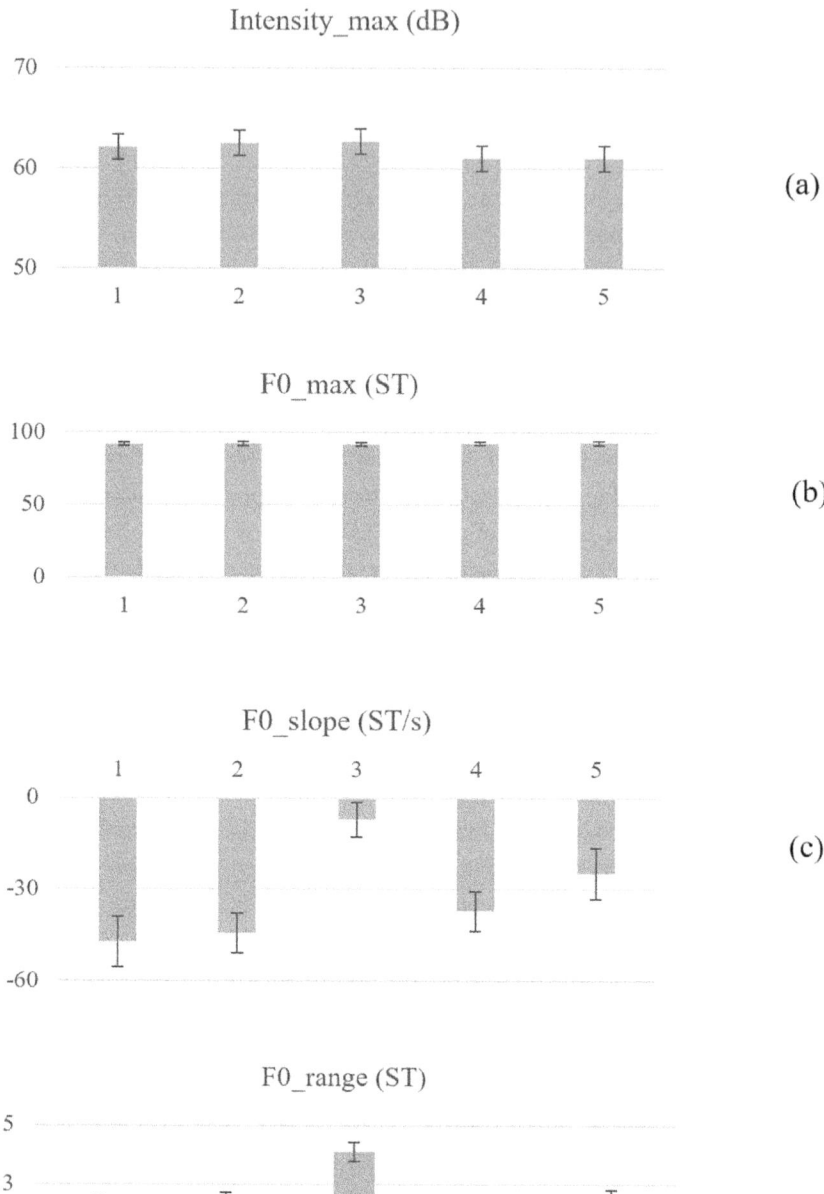

Figure 12 Estimated mean values of (a) maximum intensity, (b) maximum standardised F0, (c) F0 slope, (d) F0 range in trisyllabic words, divided by the stress condition: 1 – initial rhythmic, 2 – pretonic, 3 – lexical stress, 4 – posttonic, 5 – final rhythmic.

Issues in Metrical Phonology 45

Table 6 Relationship between metrical structure and phonetic form

Left side		Right side	
Phonological structure	Phonetic form	Phonological structure	Phonetic form
a. ˌσσˈσ	(a)	d. ˈσσˌσ	(d)
b. ˌσσσˈσ	(b)	e. ˈσσσˌσ	(e)
c. ˌσσˌσσˈσ	(c)	f. ˈσσˌσσˌσ	(f)

structure assumed by the metrical theory (cf. Section 2.1.2) is not fully expressed on the phonetic level. In particular, metrical theory predicts a symmetrical bidirectional pattern of the distribution of rhythmic stress in the positions preceding and following lexical stress. Yet, the acoustic measurements show that only the metrical positions to the right of lexical stress exhibit a predicted pattern, whereas at the opposite side – that is, in the positions to the left of lexical stress – rhythmic beats appear phonetically only in words in which lexical stress is removed from the left word edge by at least four syllables. This is schematically illustrated in Table 6, in which we juxtapose, for ease of comparison, words of different lengths with lexical stress placed on the final (left-hand column) and initial (right-hand column) syllables. The graphs represent length in relative, not absolute terms. As our previous studies of words with initial lexical stress were based on entire syllables, for the purpose of creating the graphs in (e) and (f), we conducted vowel duration measurements based on our database from twelve speakers. We selected analogous items [ˈbat͡ʃitiˌmɛ] 'see, 3rd pers. sg. future', [ˈʋisipaˌti] 'spill out, inf.', [ˈpadatiˌmɛ] 'fall, 3rd pers. sg. future' and [ˈbat͡ʃiˌtimɛˌtɛ] 'see, 2nd pers. pl. future', [ˈʋisiˌpatiˌsʲa] 'spill out, inf. refl.', [ˈpadaˌtimɛˌtɛ] 'fall, 2nd pers. pl. future' for (e) and (f), respectively, occurring in three repetitions each. The second and the third syllables are balanced in terms of the number of occurrences of the low vowel [a] and the high vowel [ɨ], so that the temporal relationship between those two syllables, different in (e) and (f) because of the iterative rhythmic status of the third syllable in (f), does not result from the intrinsic differences in length between low and high vowels.

To summarise briefly, edge-based rhythmic stress has been detected in all word types with lexical stress at the left word edge (d–f). In contrast, if lexical stress is located at the right word edge, then rhythmic stress is acoustically present only in longer words – that is, in (c), but not in (a) and (b). We have demonstrated in previous sections that the asymmetry in the leftward versus rightward pattern is caused by the presence of the lengthening of the pretonic syllable. As illustrated in the left-hand column in Table 6, there is a subtle but consistent increase in duration in the pretonic syllable in words with lexical stress on the third, fourth, and fifth syllables. The comparison of the temporal patterns across the first two syllables in [ˌσσˈσ] words in (a) with [ˌσσˌσσˈσ] words in (c) reveals that the initial syllables in [ˌσσˈσ] words do not resemble the initial [ˌσσ-] pattern of [ˌσσˌσσˈσ] words. Rather, they show the gradual lengthening effect in the vicinity of lexical stress as in the pretonic positions in [ˌσσ,**σσ**ˈσ]. Durational enhancement of the pretonic syllable also prevails in [ˌσσσˈσ] words in (b), in which we did not detect durationally based initial rhythmic stress. Interestingly, this temporal pattern parallels the timing structure detected in the positions preceding lexical stress in longer words with the lapse [ˌσσ,**σσσ**ˈσ], discussed earlier in Section 2.2.2. Thus, it appears that a distance of at least four syllables between the left edge of the word and the lexical stress-bearing syllable is required for the phonetic (duration-based) manifestation of rhythmic stress to be possible. In Section 3, we address the question of whether this timing pattern can be accounted for in a principled way (based on phonological representation) or, rather, should be relegated to the realm of phonetic implementation.

In light of our results, a question arises as to whether secondary stress in (a) and (b) in Table 6 should be represented in transcription. A reviewer suggests to omit secondary stresses when they are not expressed phonetically. In this scenario, words such as [ˌmafiaˈzin] 'shop, nom. sg.' and [ˌpɛrɛkɔˈnaʊ] 'persuade, past. masc.' would be transcribed [mafiaˈzin] 'shop, nom. sg.' and [pɛrɛkɔˈnaʊ] – that is, without initial rhythmic stresses. This transcription, though being more accurate from the phonetic point of view, would miss an important generalisation about the nature of rhythmic stress. As we discuss in Section 3.2, the absence of a phonetic cue to secondary stress in these cases is not governed by some additional rhythmic principles, but rather is caused by the presence of the lexical stress domain which hinders the acoustic expression of rhythmic prominence. In order to reflect the fact that this phonetically unexpressed stress is phonologically present as it interacts with the lexical stress domain, we retain the transcription of secondary stress in shorter words schematised in (a) and (b) in Table 6.

3 Discussion and Directions for Future Research

In this section, we demonstrate that the Ukrainian data significantly contribute to the development of metrical theory – by shedding new light on the character and extent of the interaction between the lexical and grammatical (rhythmic) stress domains within a hybrid phonological system, and, what is equally important, by improving our understanding of the complex relationship between categorical and gradient (duration-based) phenomena. The discussion is divided into three parts. In Section 3.1, an argument is presented for the necessity of restoring licencing rhythmic constraints (LAPSE-AT-PEAK) as part of the universal grammar, in accordance with the previous discussion in Mołczanow and Łukaszewicz (2021). In Section 3.2, the argument concerning the nature of the interaction between grammatical (rhythmic) and lexical stress domains is further developed on the basis of the phonetic asymmetry in temporal patterns occurring to the left and to the right of the lexical stress position. A typological link with the well-known pretonic lengthening phenomena in East Slavic is provided. In Section 3.3, we propose a formal representational model of lexical stress, which not only allows us to predict the interaction between lexical and grammatical stress, but also to successfully integrate the phonological and phonetic domains. In this model, the location of primary stress is specified lexically and serves as the landmark for the propagation of rhythmic stress – formally, the lexical stress position falls within the purview of the rhythmic constraint, LAPSE-AT-PEAK; at the same time, the domain of phonetic manifestation of lexical stress is defined with reference to a boundary demarcated by rhythmic beats.

3.1 Mirror Image Rhythmic Stress Patterns: An Argument for Rhythmic Licencing

In this Element, we have adduced extensive empirical data on the metrical structure of Ukrainian, a hybrid metrical system combining unpredictable lexical stress and grammatical iterative secondary stress. Synthesising the new findings with previous empirical work, we have argued that the Ukrainian metrical system poses a challenge for current theories employing the mechanism of gradient alignment and/or generating rhythmic prominences on the basis of metrical feet. In accordance with previous formal analyses of the Ukrainian system (Łukaszewicz & Mołczanow 2019; Mołczanow & Łukaszewicz 2021), we suggest an alternative account based on licencing theories that appeal directly to the metrical grid.

The metrical system of Ukrainian has been shown to accommodate mirror-image stress patterns, such as [ˈσσˌσσˌσ] versus [ˌσσˌσσˈσ], [σˈσσˌσ] versus [ˌσσˈσσ], et cetera, which makes it a special case of metrical bidirectionality. Whereas in other bidirectional stress systems (e.g. Polish, Garawa), the iteration of rhythmic stresses proceeds in one direction – that is, from the left or right edge towards the opposite edge where the primary stress is located – in Ukrainian, it can proceed in two directions simultaneously. This is because

Ukrainian has free lexical stress, not primary stress bound to one of the word's edges by a grammatical principle. This characteristic of the Ukrainian system helps clarify the nature of the relationship between primary and secondary stress in bidirectional stress systems. The formal apparatus on which most accounts of bidirectional stress systems have been based involves gradient alignment, which has an effect of orienting rhythmic prominences with respect to word edges, rather than relative to the primary stress. This mechanism fails to generate correct results for the hybrid system of Ukrainian because it pushes all rhythmic stresses either towards the left edge, thus correctly for [ˌσσˌσσσˈσ] words, but incorrectly for [ˈσσσˌσσˌσ] words, or the right edge – correctly for [ˈσσσˌσσˌσ] words and incorrectly for [ˌσσˌσσσˈσ] words. As initially observed by Mołczanow and Łukaszewicz (2021: 573), such directionality paradoxes point to the primary stress acting as the landmark towards which rhythmic stresses propagate from both edges (as in polar rhythm systems predicted in van der Hulst 1996, 2012, 2014); the exclusively leftward or exclusively rightward orientation of rhythmic stress iteration is not supported by the Ukrainian data.

The Ukrainian data require that rhythmic stresses are 'repelled' from primary stress in both directions rather than being pushed to the left edge or to the right edge. This 'repelling' or 'radiation' effect of the primary stress will produce lapses in the vicinity of the peak in metrical strings containing an odd number of syllables, which is formally expressed in terms of the licencing constraint, LAPSE-AT-PEAK (Kager 2001). By referring to the primary stress as the licensor, LAPSE-AT-PEAK hinges on the difference in status between the primary and rhythmic stress. Notably, this difference is also highlighted in the parameter-based approach of van der Hulst (1996, 2012, 2014), but rendered irrelevant in technical solutions aimed at orienting all metrical structure with respect to edges of the word (see e.g. Hyde 2002, 2016 and Martínez-Paricio & Kager 2015). In purely grammatical stress systems, in which the primary stress is necessarily fixed relative to one of the word's edges, it is impossible to disentangle the potential demarcating effect of primary stress from that of the corresponding word edge because they coincide. It is thus impossible to unambiguously point to the adequate mechanism governing the rhythmic stress propagation pattern – that is, whether it should be licencing with respect to the peak or, rather, gradient alignment with respect to the designated word edge. The confound does not exist in Ukrainian because it has free lexical stress. The role of lexical stress as a demarcating factor in rhythmic stress propagation is self-evident in Ukrainian: rhythmic stresses appear only when the distance between the primary stress and the edge of the word is sufficiently big to accommodate these stresses. Lexical stress and rhythmic stress have a different status as they are located in different components, lexical versus grammatical. Primary stress, being lexically specified, is insensitive to the presence of rhythmic stress and is not influenced by its position. In contrast, the application of rhythmic stress crucially depends on the position of lexical stress relative to the edge of the word.

The propagation of rhythmic stress in Ukrainian has been analysed in terms of prominences specified directly on the metrical grid, without appealing to metrical feet. It seems that from the point of view of rhythmic stress, the metrical grid representation not only provides a sufficient analytical environment, but also helps circumvent some insurmountable difficulties arising in foot-based accounts. Among those are making arbitrary (or even contradictory) assumptions concerning the left-headed (trochaic) or right-headed (iambic) foot parsing, predicting the conditions in which degenerate feet could occur or ruling out fully parsed optimal outputs such as *[(ˈlafiɔ)(ˌditɨ)(ˌmɛtɛ)], with respect to which the correct output [(ˈlafiɔ)dɨ(ˌtimɛ)(ˌtɛ)] remains suboptimal. Also, an attempt at building metrical feet on the basis of phonologically encoded duration is not an empirically adequate solution, as it makes incorrect predictions from the point of view of other aspects of the Ukrainian system, involving phonological length (geminate vs. consonantal cluster vs. singleton phonology). This is not to say that feet can be entirely dispensed with in phonological analysis. There is a considerable body of evidence across the world's languages on the interaction between metrical and segmental phenomena in which foot-sized constituents play an essential role; consider, for example, vowel reduction in Dutch (Booij 1995), flapping in English (Kiparsky 1979), and glottal stop insertion in German (Wiese 1996), to mention just a few. The lack of stress-independent evidence for foot structure in Slavic languages taps into the perennial debate on the availability of all phonetic features and structures in every language. As has been standardly assumed, the domains which constitute the prosodic hierarchy are universally present in linguistic systems (Nespor & Vogel 1986). However, there is ample evidence that not all prosodic units play the same role in the phonological description of individual languages. Hyman (1983, 2011), for instance, argues that syllabic constituents are redundant in Gokana, whose system can be more insightfully analysed employing moras. However, rather than denying the syllable a legitimate theoretical status, he suggests that 'languages differ in the nature and extent of the "activation" of phonological properties' (Hyman 2011: 55). This argument is echoed in Mołczanow and Łukaszewicz (2021: 573), who, based on the Ukrainian data, suggest that languages differ in whether feet or grids are selected as primary building blocks of prosodic structure. Since Ukrainian opts for a grid structure assigned with reference to word edges, the prosodic word appears to be more important than the foot, which seems to be less 'activated' in this language.[8] We resort to foot-based constituency in our discussion concerning the lexical stress representation in Ukrainian in Section 3.3. The proposed model of lexical stress representation will allow us to account for the ideal symmetry between the leftward and rightward rhythmic stress iteration patterns, as predicted by the metrical theory equipped with the licencing constraint LAPSE-AT-PEAK, but also for the phonetic asymmetry caused by pretonic lengthening, which we discuss in Section 3.2.

3.2 The Phonetic Asymmetry: Pretonic Lengthening as the Lexical Stress Domain Extension

The results of acoustic studies, presented in Sections 2.2 and 2.3, demonstrate an interesting phonetic asymmetry between the metrical structures to the left and to the right of lexical stress in Ukrainian. As schematised in Table 6, the temporal patterns to the right of lexical stress consistently correspond to the alternating rhythm of stressed and unstressed syllables – they proceed from the end of the word towards the lexical stress position, with lapses adjacent to lexical stress, as predicted by LAPSE-AT-PEAK. The presence of enhanced duration in metrically strong positions has been confirmed on the basis of longer words, such as [ˈbat͡ʃitiˌmɛtɛˌsʲa] 'see, 2nd pers. refl. pl. future' (Łukaszewicz & Mołczanow 2018a), as well as shorter words, such as [ˈt͡ʃɛrɛˌpa] 'skull, gen. sg.', whose length is minimal from the point of view of accommodating rhythmic stress. The existence of an alternating pattern of stressed and unstressed syllables has also been confirmed for metrical strings occurring to the left of lexical stress: in words such as [ˌtɛlɛˌfɔnʲizuˈvati] 'to set up telephone connection, inf.', both the initial and third (metrically strong) syllables are longer than the second (weak) syllable (Łukaszewicz & Mołczanow 2018b), again in accordance with LAPSE-AT-PEAK. However, as originally observed in Łukaszewicz and Mołczanow (2018b), there is also a gradual lengthening effect across the prosodic positions preceding lexical stress; as a result, the alternating strong-weak pattern is seen to disappear in the vicinity of lexical stress.

The phenomenon of pretonic lengthening in Ukrainian has been conceived of as a lexical stress domain effect unconnected with rhythm (Łukaszewicz & Mołczanow 2018b: 378).[9] A similarly gradient lengthening pattern across the syllables preceding lexical stress has been reported for words with lexical stress on the sixth ([ˌσσˌσσσˈσ(σ)]), fifth ([ˌσσˌσσˈσ(σ)]), and fourth syllables [ˌσσσˈσ(σ)]

---

[8] We are grateful to an anonymous reviewer for this suggestion.
[9] A comparable interpretation of pretonic lengthening as the extension of the lexical stress domain has been put forward by Borise (2015), who has proposed a disyllabic stress domain for the Aŭciuki dialect of Belarusian.

(Łukaszewicz & Mołczanow 2018b). A recent acoustic study of temporal patterns in [ˌσσˌσσ'σ(σ)] and [ˌσσσ'σ(σ)] words (Łukaszewicz et al. submitted) reveals an important difference in the rendition of the initial rhythmically stressed syllable, which seems to be connected with the scope of the pretonic lengthening effect. In [ˌσσσ'σ(σ)] words, as well as in shorter words of the [ˌσσ'σ] type, for which novel acoustic data were presented in Section 2.3, the initial syllable does not exhibit a significantly increased duration despite being metrically strong. In contrast, temporal enhancement on the initial syllable has been detected in words where the distance between lexical stress and the word edge is of at least four syllables – that is, in ([ˌσσˌσσ'σ(σ)] and [ˌσσˌσσσ'σ(σ)]) words. What those words have in common is the presence of rhythmic stress iteration, resulting in an additional marking of the rhythmic beat on the third syllable. This is an important observation from the point of view of determining the scope of the lexical domain extension. It indicates that pretonic lengthening, which has an inhibitory effect on the duration-based expression of rhythmic stress, extends from the lexical stress position to the nearest preceding rhythmic beat. Being a lexical domain effect, pretonic lengthening does not fall within the purview of the rhythmic constraint LAPSE-AT-PEAK; however, it is precisely through the operation of this constraint that the position of metrical beats vis-à-vis the lexical stress position is determined, which, in turn, specifies the scope of the lexical stress domain extension on the phonetic level.

Considering the Ukrainian pretonic lengthening pattern from the typological perspective of East Slavic, the phenomenon in Ukrainian seems to be very subtle relative to that reported for some East Slavic dialects. According to Bethin (2006), pretonic lengthening in East Slavic dialects is caused by High tone, associated with a syllable immediately preceding the primary stress. Mołczanow (2022) further argues that High tone compels the lowering of the pretonic vowel in East Slavic dialects which have phonological vowel reduction. However, there is no evidence for the presence of High tone in the pretonic position in Ukrainian. Phonetically, F0 measurements reported in Łukaszewicz and Mołczanow (2018b, 2018c), as well as in the current study based on trisyllabic words, do not reveal any F0 rise associated with the pretonic syllable. Also, there are no phonological effects, comparable to the categorical change of pretonic vowels in some East Slavic dialect, which would justify postulating High tone as a diacritic feature in Ukrainian.

A well-studied case of pretonic lengthening is Standard Russian. As mentioned in Section 1.3, Russian has different degrees of vowel reduction: non-categorical (phonetic) reduction in the second pretonic position versus categorical (phonological) reduction in the first pretonic position, accompanied by lengthening occurring in that position (Barnes 2006). Ukrainian is different in this regard: formant measurements point to a reduced quality of the vowel [a] in all positions following or preceding lexical stress, thus confirming the presence of phonetic vowel reduction in Ukrainian. Barnes (2006) reports a strong correlation between F1 and duration in the second pretonic but not in the pretonic position in Russian. The results of our study of Ukrainian words having the structure [ˌσσσˈσ(σ)] point to a reverse pattern: it is the first pretonic position which shows the greatest amount of correlation between the undershoot of F1 targets and decreasing duration. The initial rhythmically stressed position exhibits stable F1 targets, which might point to phonologisation of this reduction pattern. As has been tentatively suggested in Łukaszewicz et al. (submitted), the reduction pattern in the metrically strong initial position may no longer be duration-dependent and may be consistently effected with lower F1 targets regardless of the available time. Although the stability of F1 targets vis-à-vis the temporal dimension has not been confirmed on the basis of trisyllabic words having the structure [ˌσσˈσ], notably, also in such words F1 targets have been detected to be considerably reduced in the rhythmic stress position relative to the pretonic vowel in the initial position in [σˈσσ] words.

In Section 3.3, we turn to the problem of formalising the lexical domain effect, with the goal of integrating the lexical and grammatical stress domains, as well as connecting the phonological and phonetic levels of linguistic description.

3.3 Formal Representation of Lexical Stress: An Integrative Approach

As we have seen throughout this Element, Ukrainian combines free lexical stress with predictable grammatical stress. Both phenomena, lexical and grammatical stress, have been extensively discussed in the literature, albeit in a different analytical context. In the case of grammatical stress systems, the research agenda is mainly centred around building models which would generate attested metrical patterns; compare the debate around the Polish stress on whether foot-based (McCarthy & Prince 1993; Hayes 1995; Kraska-Szlenk 2003) or grid-based (Rubach & Booij 1985) mechanisms should be employed in the analysis of this system. The same question has been posed in the previous analysis of the Ukrainian rhythmic stress (Mołczanow & Łukaszewicz 2021), as discussed in Sections 2.1.2 and 3.1. This debate is secondary from the point of view of lexical stress modelling, which is not so much concerned with the tools assigning stress to a given position within a word but rather aims to establish how the accentual properties are represented in the lexicon and what mechanisms are involved in relating the underlying representation of accent and its surface manifestation.[10]

The representation of lexical stress has been the subject of much theoretical discussion. Various types of devices have been proposed in the literature, including a diacritic feature marking (Melvold 1990), parentheses (Halle 1997), a floating autosegmental feature (Revithiadou 1999), and a metrical grid (Halle & Vergnaud 1987; Idsardi 1992; Alderete 1999; Mołczanow 2022).[11] All these mechanisms can in principle be employed to represent Ukrainian lexical stress. However, we argue in Mołczanow and Łukaszewicz (2021) that rhythmic stress in Ukrainian can be most successfully derived using the grid-based model of representation. Thus formalising the lexical representation of the accent in Ukrainian as 'a prominence on the metrical grid' (Alderete 1999: 16) allows for a coherent analysis of both lexical and grammatical (rhythmic) stress. On this view, the grid mark on Level 2 in (10) comes from the underlying representation, whereas syllabic and rhythmic structure is generated by the grammar.

(10) a. *Underlying representation*
       x
/munʲit͡sɨpalʲitɛt/

  b. *Surface representation*
                 x   Level 2 (primary stress)
    x . x . . x   Level 1 (secondary stress)
    x x x x x x   Level 0 (syllable positions)
[ˌmunʲi ˌt͡sɨpalʲi'tɛt]

The grammar ensures that the lexically encoded prominence on the grid is realised as the head of the prosodic word in the output representation. In terms of the OT apparatus, lexically specified accents surface on the corresponding vowels in the output due to the prosodic constraint NO-FLOP-PROM ('Corresponding prominences must have corresponding sponsors and links'; Alderete 1999: 18), which preserves a faithful mapping between the position of prominence in the underlying and surface structure.

It has been standardly assumed that in lexical stress systems, in addition to a grid mark on Level 2 (cf. (10b)), lexical prominence is structurally represented

---

[10] Following a long-established tradition (e.g. Abercrombie 1976; Fox 2000; van der Hulst 2011), we use the term 'accent' to refer to an underlying prosodic feature and the term 'stress' to refer to the surface representation of metrical prominence.

[11] In the context of Slavic, most analyses have been developed based on Russian. The scope of the present Element does not allow us to present a detailed review of various proposals, but see Fox (2000) for general discussion, Bethin (1998) for an overview of the representation of accentual properties in Slavic languages, and Revithiadou (1999) for a review of different analyses developed for Russian.

as a headed foot constructed with reference to the lexically accented vowel (e.g. Halle & Vergnaud 1987). For instance, a right-headed non-exhaustive footing has been proposed for Russian by Halle and Vergnaud (1987), Melvold (1990), Alderete (1995), Crosswhite (2001), Crosswhite et al. (2003), and Mołczanow (2022). That is, only one foot per word is built – for example, [fə(naˈlo)gʲɪjə] 'phonology, nom. sg.' – in that language. The grouping of the tonic and the pretonic syllables into one constituent allows us to explain the asymmetry in the distribution of vowel reduction in this language.[12]

We have previously suggested that the domain of lexical stress in Ukrainian extends to positions preceding lexical stress, as evidenced by the asymmetrical distribution of secondary stresses to the right and to the left from primary stress. Based on the presence of pretonic lengthening, one could assume that, similarly to Russian, Ukrainian builds an iambic foot over the pretonic and the tonic syllables – for example, [ˌfɔ(nɔˈlɔ)ɦʲiˌja] 'phonology, nom. sg.'. This footing, however, while correctly predicting pretonic lengthening in the syllable immediately preceding lexical stress, fails to account for the gradual lengthening effect across two prosodic positions preceding lexical stress in [ˌσσˈσ] and [ˌσσˌσσˈσ] and three prosodic positions in [ˌσσσˈσ] and [ˌσσˌσσσˈσ] (cf. Figure 5 and Table 6).

As we observed in Section 3.2, pretonic lengthening extends from the lexical stress position to the nearest preceding rhythmic stress. This generalisation can be formally expressed if we assume that a maximally binary right-headed constituent is built over the grid positions at Level 2, yielding the structures in (11).

(11) The lexical stress domain

a. (.   x)   Level 2 (primary stress)
   .   x   Level 1 (secondary stress)
   x   x   Level 0 (syllable positions)
   σ   ˈσ

b. (.   x)   Level 2 (primary stress)
   x   .   x   Level 1 (secondary stress)
   x   x   x   Level 0 (syllable positions)
  ˌσ   σ ˈσ

c. (.   x)   Level 2 (primary stress)
   x   .   . x   Level 1 (secondary stress)
   x   x   x x   Level 0 (syllable positions)
  ˌσ   σ   σ ˈσ

---

[12] Russian has a two-degree vowel reduction, with different sets of vowels found in pretonic and atonic syllables – for example, in the /fonoˈlogija/ [fə(naˈlo)gʲɪjə] 'phonology, nom. sg.', /o/ is reduced to [ə] in the initial syllable and to [a] in the pretonic syllable (see Mołczanow 2022 for further discussion).

d. .   (.   x)   Level 2 (primary stress)
    x   .   x   .   x   Level 1 (secondary stress)
    x   x   x   x   x   Level 0 (syllable positions)
    ˌσ σ   ˌσ σ   ˈσ

e. .   (.   x) Level 2 (primary stress)
    x   .   x   .   .   x   Level 1 (secondary stress)
    x   x   x   x   x   x   Level 0 (syllable positions)
    ˌσ σ   ˌσ σ   σ   ˈσ

In words with lexically stressed second syllable, a constituent is erected over the grid corresponding to lexical stress and the pretonic position (11a). When lexical stress is separated from the left word edge by two or more syllables (11b–11e), the boundary of the right-headed constituent is determined by the position of the nearest secondary stress: in shorter words in (11b) and (11c), the leftward edge of the domain of lexical stress coincides with the left word edge, whereas in longer words in (11d) and (11e), the leftward edge of the lexical stress domain coincides with the position of the iterative rhythmic beat.[13] This model allows us to delimit the domain of the leftward expansion of lexical stress and thus to account for the absence of strong/weak alternation of rhythmic beats in the initial and second positions in (11b) and (11c) and across the iterative and the following syllable(s) in (11d) and (11e). Initial stress is acoustically salient in (11d) and (11e) because the first and the second syllables lie outside the purview of the domain of lexical stress.

Another issue which should be mentioned in connection with the phonological modelling of lexical stress is its interaction with morphology. It was pointed out in Section 2.1.1 that, similarly to other East Slavic languages, there exist several morphologically conditioned accentual paradigms in Ukrainian, listed in (12) (cf. Table 1).[14]

(12) a. stems with stress fixed on one of the syllables of the stem in all forms, e.g. [rɔˈdin+a] 'family, nom. sg.' – [rɔˈdin+ɨ] 'id., nom. pl.'

---

[13] A reviewer asks whether the domain of lengthening could be a superfoot. In this scenario, lengthening would target the initial domain in a foot – for example, [(σ₃ (σ₂ σ₁))], [(σ₄ (σ₃ (σ₂ ˈσ₁)))], and the innermost foot would display the greater lengthening effect. This analysis is problematic for two reasons. First, it incorrectly predicts that σ₄ and σ₃ should exhibit different degrees of lengthening. Second, the number of iterative feet has to be stipulated not to exceed three, otherwise rhythmic stress will not appear in longer words, as in *[(σ₅ (σ₄ (σ₃ (σ₂ ˈσ₁))))]. Let us also point out that postulating internally layered binary and ternary feet (Martínez-Paricio & Kager 2015) is not an option either as this analysis runs into a number of ranking paradoxes when applied to the Ukrainian data (Mołczanow and Łukaszewicz 2021; see also fn. 3).

[14] For further discussion of the accentual paradigms of Ukrainian see Stankiewicz (1993) and Butska (2002). Both the historical evolution and the present-day state of the accentual system of East Slavic have been extensively discussed in the literature (see e.g. Jakobson, 1963; Halle, 1973; Kiparsky & Halle, 1977; Zaliznjak, 1985; Melvold, 1990; Mołczanow et al. 2013, 2019a; Stankiewicz 1993, among many others).

b. stress fixed on the inflectional ending (when present) in all forms, e.g. [ʒittʲ+ˈa] 'life, nom. sg.' – [ʒittʲ+ˈi] 'id., loc. pl.'
c. mobile stress, with stress alternating between stem and inflection, e.g. [nɔʋɨn+ˈa] 'news, nom. sg.' – [nɔˈʋɨn+ɨ] 'id., nom. pl.'

Based on their accentual properties, East Slavic morphemes (both stems and affixes) are traditionally classified as accented and unaccented (Jakobson 1963; Halle 1973; Kiparsky & Halle 1977; Zaliznjak 1985). In accented morphemes, accent is lexically specified on one of the vowels, whereas in unaccented morphemes, accent is not encoded in the underlying representation, and surface stress is derived by grammar. There has been an ongoing debate in the literature concerning the specification of accent in stems with stress fixed on the inflectional ending (12b) and in stems with mobile stress (12c). If both (12b) and (12c) are unaccented in the underlying representation, then two different lexically indexed rules need to be postulated to derive surface forms. If only one type is unaccented, then only one rule is needed, but the question remains why this type and not the other is chosen to be represented as unaccented in the lexicon.[15] This issue is extraneous from the point of view of the present study, as the choice of a particular model of representation of accented and unaccented stems does not affect the core of the present discussion, which concentrates on (i) the interaction between lexical and rhythmic stress and (ii) the relation between phonological categories and their phonetic manifestation. Let us note, however, that previous experimental studies on Russian employing encephalographic and aphasic data (Mołczanow et al. 2013, Mołczanow et al. 2019a) have not found convincing evidence for the claim that accented and unaccented stems are represented differently in the lexicon; thus it can be assumed that both are lexically specified. To the best of our knowledge, no such studies have been conducted with Ukrainian speakers, so this issue cannot be resolved at present and thus awaits future investigation.

Needless to say, more empirical research is also needed on the phonetics of the prosodic system of Ukrainian. One of the questions that future studies of Ukrainian should address is the effect of metrical prominence on the relationship between the temporal dimension and formant structure, depending on a vowel category. Also, little is known about the potential effect of polysyllabic shortening or varying speech rates on the rendition of stress in Ukrainian. These important aspects of the temporal dimension should also be addressed in future research.

---

[15] In traditional analyses, stems in (12b) have been specified as post-accenting in the lexicon. An in-depth discussion of the issues related to lexical representation of stress is beyond the scope of the present study, as the literature on this subject is vast; for the analysis of Ukrainian, see Butska (2002) and Steriade and Yanovich (2015), for Russian, see Halle (1973, 1997), Melvold (1990), Idsardi (1992), Alderete (1999) Revithiadou 1999), Mołczanow et al. (2013, 2019a).

To conclude, we hope that the present Element has shed new light on general mechanisms underlying the interaction between lexical and grammatical stress domains as well as on the relationship between the phonology and phonetics of stress. Seen through the complexities of the prosodic system of Ukrainian, not all apparently comparable mechanisms of stress assignment turn out equally adequate. Specifically, we have argued for the necessity of restoring rhythmic licencing constraints (such as Lapse-at-Peak) as a universal mechanism governing the directionality of rhythmic stress assignment. Also, directionality paradoxes caused by the Ukrainian mirror-image stress patterns can be accounted for if grid- rather than foot-based representations are assumed. Such representations also allow us to propose a coherent model of the interaction between lexical and rhythmic stress, in which the location of primary stress is specified lexically, but the domain of its phonetic manifestation is defined depending on the position of rhythmic beats represented in terms of grids. The proposed model of lexical stress representation allows us to account for the phonological symmetry between the leftward and rightward rhythmic stress iteration patterns and for the phonetic asymmetry caused by pretonic lengthening.

References

Abercrombie, D. (1965/71). *Syllable Quantities and Enclitics in English: Studies in Phonetics and Linguistics.* 3rd ed. Oxford: Oxford University Press.

Abercrombie, D. (1976). Stress and some other terms. *Work in Progress*, **9**, 51–3. (Rpt. in D. Abercrombie (1991). *Fifty Years in Phonetics.* Edinburgh: Edinburgh University Press).

Agwuele, A., Sussman, H. M. & Lindblom, B. (2008). The effect of speaking rate on consonant vowel coarticulation. *Phonetica*, **65**, 194–209.

Alber, B. (2005). Clash, lapse and directionality. *Natural Language and Linguistic Theory*, **23**, 485–542.

Alderete, J. (1995). Faithfulness to prosodic heads. Rutgers Optimality Archive, Report No. 94.

Alderete, J. (1999). Morphologically governed accent in Optimality Theory. PhD dissertation, University of Massachusetts.

Barnes, J. (2006). *Strength and Weakness at the Interface: Positional Neutralization in Phonetics and Phonology.* Berlin: Mouton de Gruyter.

Beckman, M. E. (1986). *Stress and Non-stress Accent.* Dordrecht: Foris.

Beckman, M. E. & Edwards, J. (1990). Lengthenings and shortenings and the nature of prosodic constituency. In J. Kingston and M. Beckman, eds., *Papers in Laboratory Phonology I: Between the Grammar and Physics of Speech.* Cambridge: Cambridge University Press, pp. 179–200.

Beckman, M. E., Edwards, J. & Fletcher, J. (1992). Prosodic structure and tempo in a sonority model of articulatory dynamics. In G. Docherty and D. R. Ladd, eds., *Papers in Laboratory Phonology II: Gesture, Segment, Prosody.* Cambridge: Cambridge University Press, pp. 68–86.

Beinum, K. & Jeannette, F. (1980). Vowel contrast reduction: An acoustic and perceptual study of Dutch vowels in various speech conditions. PhD dissertation, University of Amsterdam.

Bethin, C. Y. (1992). Iotation and gemination in Ukrainian. *The Slavic and East European Journal*, **36**, 275–301.

Bethin, C. Y. (1998). *Slavic Prosody: Language Change and Phonological Theory.* Cambridge: Cambridge University Press.

Bethin, C. Y. (2006). Stress and tone in East Slavic dialects. *Phonology*, **23**(2), 125–156.

Bilodid, I. K. (1969). *Sučasna ukrajins'ka literaturna mova. Vstup. Fonetyka.* Kyiv: Naukova Dumka.

References

Boersma, P. & Weenink, D. (1992–2022). Praat: Doing phonetics by computer. Computer program. www.praat.org.

Booij, G. (1995). *The Phonology of Dutch*. Oxford: Oxford University Press.

Borise, L. (2015). Prominence redistribution in the Aŭciuki dialect of Belarusian. In Y. Oseki, M. Esipova, and S. Harves, eds., *Proceedings of the 24th Meeting of Formal Approaches to Slavic Linguistics*. Ann Arbor: Michigan Slavic Publications, pp. 94–109.

Broch, O. (1910). *Očerk fiziologii slavjanskoj reči*. St. Petersburg: Tipografija imperatorskoj akademii nauk.

Brovčenko, T. O. (1969). *Slovesnyj naholos v sučasnij ukrajins'kij movi: Eksperymental'ne doslidžennja*. Kyiv: Naukova Dumka.

Buckley, E. (2009). Locality in metrical typology. *Phonology*, **26**(3), 389–435.

Butska, L. (2002). Faithful stress in paradigms: Nominal inflection in Ukrainian and Russian. PhD dissertation, Rutgers University.

Chitoran, I. & Hualde, J. I. (2007). From hiatus to diphthong: The evolution of vowel sequences in Romance. *Phonology*, **24**(1), 37–75.

Chomsky, N. & Halle, M. (1968). *The Sound Pattern of English*. New York: Harper and Row.

Cohen, E., Silber-Varod, V. & Amir, N. (2018). The acoustics of primary and secondary stress in Modern Hebrew. *Brill's Journal of Afroasiatic Languages and Linguistics*, **10**(1), 5–23.

Crosswhite, K. (2001). *Vowel Reduction in Optimality Theory*. New York: Routledge.

Crosswhite, K., Alderete, J., Beasley, T. & Markman, V. (2003). Morphological effects on default stress placement in novel Russian words. *Proceedings of the West Coast Conference on Formal Linguistics*, **22**, 151–164.

Czekman, W. & Smułkowa, E. (1988). *Fonetyka i fonologia języka białoruskiego z elementami fonetyki i fonologii ogólnej*. Warszawa: Państwowe Wydawnictwo Naukowe.

Delattre, P. (1965). *Comparing the Phonetic Features of English, French, German and Spanish*. Heidelberg: Julius Groos.

Elenbaas, N. & Kager, R. (1999). Ternary rhythm and the lapse constraint. *Phonology*, **16**(3), 273–329.

Flege, J. E. (1988). Effects of speaking rate on tongue position and velocity of movement in vowel production. *Journal of the Acoustical Society of America*, **84**(3), 901–916.

Flemming, E. S. (2004). Contrast and perceptual distinctiveness. In B. Hayes, R. Kirchner and D. Steriade, eds., *Phonetically Based Phonology*. Cambridge: Cambridge University Press, pp. 232–276.

Fourakis, M. (1991). Tempo, stress, and vowel reduction in American English. *Journal of the Acoustical Society of America*, **90**, 1816–1827.

Fox, A. (2000). *Prosodic Features and Prosodic Structure: The Phonology of Suprasegmentals*. Oxford: Oxford University Press.

Franks, S. (1985). Extrametricality and stress in Polish. *Linguistic Inquiry*, **16**, 144–151.

Furby, Ch. (1974). *Garawa Phonology*. Canberra: Australian National University.

Garellek, M. & White, J. (2015). Phonetics of Tongan stress. *Journal of the International Phonetic Association*, **45**(1), 13–34.

Gordon, M. (2002). A factorial typology of quantity-insensitive stress. *Natural Language and Linguistic Theory*, **20**, 491–552.

Gordon, M. & Roettger, T. (2017). Acoustic correlates of word stress: A cross-linguistic survey. *Linguistics Vanguard*, **3**(1), 20170006.

Halle, M. (1973). The accentuation of Russian words. *Language*, **49**, 312–348.

Halle, M. (1997). On stress and accent in Indo-European. *Language*, **73**, 275–313.

Halle, M. & Vergnaud, J.-R. (1987). *An Essay on Stress*. Cambridge, MA: MIT Press.

Hayes, B. (1980). A metrical theory of stress rules. PhD dissertation, Massachusetts Institute of Technology.

Hayes, B. (1989). Compensatory lengthening in moraic phonology. *Linguistic Inquiry*, **20**, 253–306.

Hayes, B. (1995). *Metrical Stress Theory: Principles and Case Studies*. Chicago, IL: University of Chicago Press.

Hermans, B. (2011). The representation of stress. In M. van Oostendorp, C. J. Ewen, E. Hume and K. Rice, eds., *The Blackwell Companion to Phonology*, vol. II. Oxford: Blackwell, pp. 980–1002.

Hermes, D. J. & Rump, H. H. (1994). Perception of prominence in speech intonation induced by rising and falling pitch movements. *Journal of the Acoustical Society of America*, **96**(1), 83–92.

Hryščenko, A. P. (2002). *Sučasna ukrajins'ka literaturna mova*, 3rd ed. Kyiv: Vyšča škola.

Hulst, H. van der. (1996). Separating primary accent and secondary accent. In R. Goedemans, H. van der Hulst and E. Visch, eds., *Stress Patterns of the World, Part I*. The Hague: Holland Academic Graphics, pp. 1–26.

Hulst, H. van der. (2011). Pitch accent systems. In C. Ewen, M. van Oostendorp and K. Rice, eds., *Phonological Compendium*. Oxford: Blackwell, pp. 1003–1026.

Hulst, H. van der. (2012). Deconstructing stress. *Lingua*, **122**, 1494–1521.

Hulst, H. van der. (2014). Representing rhythm. In H. van der Hulst, ed., *Word Stress: Theoretical and Typological Issues*. Cambridge: Cambridge University Press, pp. 325–365.

Hyde, B. (2002). A restrictive theory of metrical stress. *Phonology*, **19**, 313–359.

Hyde, B. (2016). *Layering and Directionality: Metrical Stress in Optimality Theory*. London: Equinox.

Hyman, L. M. (1983). Are there syllables in Gokana? In J. Kaye, H. Koopman, D. Sportiche and A. Dugas, eds., *Current Approaches to African Linguistics: Vol. 2*. Dordrecht: Foris, pp. 171–179.

Hyman, L. M. (2011). Does Gokana really have no syllables? Or: What's so great about being universal? *Phonology*, **28**, 55–85.

Idsardi, W. (1992). The computation of prosody. PhD dissertation, Massachusetts Institute of Technology.

Jakobson, R. (1963). Opyt fonologičeskogo podxoda k istoričeskim voprosam slavjanskoj akcentologii. In *American Contributions to the 5th International Congress of Slavists, vol. I: Linguistic Contributions*. The Hague: Mouton, pp. 153–178.

Jones, D. (1923). *The Phonetics of Russian*. Revised by D. Ward, 1969. Cambridge: Cambridge University Press.

Kager, R. (2001). Rhythmic directionality by positional licensing. Paper presented at the 5th HIL Phonology Conference, Potsdam, 11 January. Available on Rutgers Optimality Archive, ROA-51.

Kager, R. (2005). Rhythmic licensing theory: An extended typology. In *Proceedings of the Third International Conference on Phonology*. Seoul: Phonology-Morphology Circle of Korea, pp. 5–31.

Kiparsky, P. (1979). Metrical structure assignment is cyclic. *Linguistic Inquiry*, **10**, 421–441.

Kiparsky, P. & Halle, M. (1977). Towards a reconstruction of the Indo-European accent. *Southern Californian Occasional Papers in Linguistics*, **1**, 209–238.

Krämer, M. (2009). *The Phonology of Italian*. Oxford: Oxford University Press.

Kraska-Szlenk, I. (2003). *The Phonology of Stress in Polish*. Munich: Lincom Europa.

Ladd, D. R. (1996). *Intonational Phonology*. New York: Cambridge University Press.

Lang-Rigal, J. (2014). A perceptual and experimental phonetic approach to dialect stereotypes. The 'tonada cordobesa' of Argentina. PhD dissertation, University of Texas at Austin.

Lehiste, I. (1970). *Suprasegmentals*. Cambridge, MA: MIT Press.

Lehr-Spławiński, T. (1916). Z fonetyki małoruskiej. *Prace Filologiczne*, **8**, 361–380.

Lenardón, M. L. (2017). Understanding the 'tonada cordobesa' from an acoustic, perceptual, and sociolinguistic perspective. PhD dissertation, University of Pittsburgh.

Liberman, M. & Prince, A. S. (1977). On stress and linguistic rhythm. *Linguistic Inquiry*, **8**, 249–336.

Lindblom, B. & Rapp, K. (1972). Reexamination of the compensatory adjustment of vowel duration in Swedish words. *Occasional Papers University of Essex*, **13**, 204–224.

Lindblom, B. (1963). Spectrographic study of vowel reduction. *Journal of the Acoustical Society of America*, **35**, 1773–1781.

Lobanov, B. M. (1971). Classification of Russian vowels spoken by different speakers. *Journal of the Acoustical Society of America*, **49**, 606–608.

Loboda, V. V. (2009). Fonetyka i fonolohija. In M. Ja. Plušč, ed., *Sučasna ukrajins'ka literaturna mova*, 7th ed. Kyiv: Vyšča škola, pp. 17–83.

Łukaszewicz, B. (2015). Polish stress revisited: Phonetic evidence of an iterative system. Paper presented at 23rd Manchester Phonology Meeting, Manchester, UK.

Łukaszewicz, B. (2018). Phonetic evidence for an iterative stress system: The issue of consonantal rhythm. *Phonology*, **35**, 115–150.

Łukaszewicz, B. & Mołczanow, J. (2018a). Leftward and rightward stress iteration in Ukrainian: Acoustic evidence and theoretical implications. In B. Czaplicki, B. Łukaszewicz and M. Opalińska, eds., *Phonology, Fieldwork and Generalizations*. Berlin: Peter Lang, pp. 259–275.

Łukaszewicz, B. & Mołczanow, J. (2018b). Rhythmic stress in Ukrainian: Acoustic evidence of a bidirectional system. *Journal of Linguistics*, **54**, 367–388.

Łukaszewicz, B. & Mołczanow, J. (2018c). The role of vowel parameters in defining lexical and subsidiary stress in Ukrainian. *Poznań Studies in Contemporary Linguistics*, **54**(3), 355–375.

Łukaszewicz, B. & Mołczanow, J. (2019). Bidirectional grammatical stress in a free lexical stress system. In E. Babatsouli, ed., *Proceedings of the International Symposium on Monolingual and Bilingual Speech 2019*, pp. 75–79.

Łukaszewicz, B. & Mołczanow, J. (2024). Word-final rhythmic prominence in Ukrainian. *Proceedings of the 12th International Conference on Speech Prosody*, pp. 285–288.

Łukaszewicz, B. & Mołczanow, J. (To appear). Metrical phonology of Slavonic stress. In N. Bermel and J. Fellerer, eds., *The Oxford Guide to the Slavonic Languages*, Oxford: Oxford University Press.

Łukaszewicz, B., Mołczanow, J. & Łukaszewicz, A. (submitted). Lexical-grammatical stress interactions: Pretonic lengthening, rhythmic stress and vowel undershoot in Ukrainian.

Łukaszewicz, B., Zajbt, E. & Krawczyk, U. (2018). The rhythm of heptasyllabic words: Evidence for metrical bidirectionality. In *Proceedings of the 9th International Conference on Speech Prosody*, pp. 676–679.

Łukaszewicz, B., Zajbt, E. & Mołczanow, J. (2020). Polish iterative stress and its phonetic parameters in quiet vs. noisy environments. *Lingua*, **240**, 102835.

Martínez-Paricio, V. & Kager, R. (2015). The binary-to-ternary rhythmic continuum in stress typology: Layered feet and non-intervention constraints. *Phonology*, **32**, 459–504.

McCarthy, J. & Prince, A. S. (1993). Generalized alignment. In G. Booij and J. van Marle, eds., *Yearbook of Morphology 1993*. Dodrecht: Kluwer, pp. 79–153.

Melvold, J. L. (1990). Structure and stress in the phonology of Russian. PhD dissertation, MIT.

Miller, J. L. (1981). Effects of speaking rate on segmental distinctions. In P. D. Eimas and J. L. Miller, eds., *Perspectives on the Study of Speech*. Hillsdale, NJ: Lawrence Erlbaum Associates, pp. 39–74.

Mołczanow, J. (2022). *Interactions of Vowel Quality and Prosody in East Slavic*. London: Equinox.

Mołczanow, J., Domahs, U., Knaus, J. & Wiese, R. (2013). The lexical representation of word stress in Russian: Evidence from event-related potentials. *The Mental Lexicon*, **8**(2), 164–194.

Mołczanow, J., Iskra, E., Dragoy, O., Wiese, R. & Domahs, U. (2019a). Default stress assignment in Russian: Evidence from acquired surface dyslexia. *Phonology*, **36**(1), 61–90.

Mołczanow, J. & Łukaszewicz, B. (2021). Metrical structure and licensing: An argument from Ukrainian. *Linguistic Inquiry*, **52**(3), 551–577.

Mołczanow, J., Łukaszewicz, B. & Łukaszewicz, A. (2018). Rhythmic stress or word-boundary effects? Comparison of primary and secondary stress correlates in segmentally identical word pairs. In *Proceedings of the 9th International Conference on Speech Prosody*, pp. 908–912.

Mołczanow, J., Łukaszewicz, B. & Łukaszewicz, A. (2019b). An acoustic study of vowel undershoot in a system with several degrees of prominence. In *Proceedings INTERSPEECH 2019*, pp. 1756–1760.

Mołczanow, J., Łukaszewicz, B. & Łukaszewicz, A. (2021). Timing patterns in a hybrid metrical system. *Lingua*, **255**, 103066.

Moon, S. J. & Lindblom, B. (1994). Interaction between duration, context, and speaking style in English stressed vowels. *Journal of the Acoustical Society of America*, **96**, 40–55.

Nadeu, M. (2014). Stress- and speech rate-induced vowel quality variation in Catalan and Spanish. *Journal of Phonetics*, **46**, 1–22.

Nakonečnyj, M. F. (1969). Naholos. In I. K. Bilodid, ed., *Sučasna ukrajins'ka literaturna mova. Vstup. Fonetyka*. Kyiv: Naukova Dumka, pp. 358–369.

Nespor, M. & Vogel, I. (1986). *Prosodic Phonology*. Dordrecht: Foris.

Nowak, P. (2006). Vowel reduction in Polish. PhD dissertation, UC Berkeley.

Osborn, H. A. (1966). Warao I: Phonology and morphophonemics. *International Journal of American Linguistics*, **32**, 108–123.

Pater, J. (2000). Nonuniformity in English secondary stress: The role of ranked and lexically specific constraints. *Phonology*, **17**, 237–274.

Plag, I., Kunter, G. & Schramm, M. (2011). Acoustic correlates of primary and secondary stress in North American English. *Journal of Phonetics*, **39**(3), 362–374.

Plušč, M. Ja. (2009). *Sučasna ukrajins'ka literaturna mova*, 7th ed. Kyiv: Vyšča škola.

Pompino-Marschall, B., Steriopolo, E. & Żygis, M. (2017). Ukrainian. *Journal of the International Phonetic Association*, 47(3), 349–357.

Prince, A. (1983). Relating to the grid. *Linguistic Inquiry*, **14**, 19–100.

Prince, A. (1990). Quantitative consequences of rhythmic organization. In K. Deaton, M. Noske and M. Ziolkowski, eds., *CLS26-II: Papers from the Parasession on the Syllable in Phonetics and Phonology*. Chicago, IL: CLS, pp. 355–398.

Revithiadou, A. (1999). Headmost accent wins: Head dominance and ideal prosodic form in lexical accent systems. PhD dissertation, Leiden.

Revithiadou, A. & Lengeris A. (2016). One or many? In search of the default stress in Greek. In J. Heinz, R. Goedemans and H. van der Hulst, eds., *Dimensions of Linguistic Stress*. Cambridge: Cambridge University Press, pp. 263–290.

Rubach, J. & Booij, G. E. (1985). A grid theory of stress in Polish. *Lingua*, **66**, 281–319.

Shevelov, G. Y. (1979). *A Historical Phonology of the Ukrainian Language*. Heidelberg: Carl Winter.

Stankiewicz, E. (1993). *The Accentual Patterns of the Slavic Languages*. Stanford, CA: Stanford University Press.

Steriade, D. & Yanovich, I. (2015). Accentual allomorphs in East Slavic: An argument for inflection dependence. In E. Bonet, M.-R. Lloret, and J. Mascaro, eds., *Understanding Allomorphy*. London: Equinox, pp. 254–313.

Steriopolo, O. I. (2012). Ukrajins'ka fonetyčna systema u paradyhmi mižnarodnoji fonetyčnoji asociaciji (MFA). *Naukovyj Visnyk Užhorods'koho Universytetu. Series*: Philology. Social communications, **27**, 51–58.

Strycharczuk, P., Ćavar, M. & Coretta, S. (2021). Distance vs time: Acoustic and articulatory consequences of reduced vowel duration in Polish. *Journal of the Acoustical Society of America*, **150**, 592–607.

Toc'ka, N. I. (1969). Zvukova charakterystyka sučasnoji ukrajins'koji literaturnoji movy. Holosni zvuky. In I. K. Bilodid, ed., *Sučasna ukrajins'ka literaturna mova. Vstup. Fonetyka*. Kyiv: Naukova Dumka, pp. 50–130.

References

Toc'ka, N. I. (1970). Nenahološeni alofony holosnyx fonem ukrajins'koji literaturnoji movy (do pytannya pro redukciju holosnyx). *Movoznavstvo*, **5**, 21–30.

Toc'ka, N. I. (1973). *Holosni fonemy ukrajins'koji literaturnoji movy.* Kyiv: Vydavnyctvo Kyjivs'koho Universytetu.

Toc'ka, N. I. (2002). Fonetyka i fonolohija. In A. P. Hryščenko, ed., *Sučasna ukrajins'ka literaturna mova*, 3rd ed. Kyiv: Vyšča škola, pp. 16–76.

Turk, A. & Shattuck-Hufnagel, S. (2007). Multiple targets of phrase-final lengthening in American English words. *Journal of Phonetics*, **35**(4), 445–472.

Turk, A. E. & Shattuck-Hufnagel, S. (2000). Word-boundary-related duration patterns in English. *Journal of Phonetics*, **28**, 397–440.

Vakulenko, M. O. (2018). Ukrainian vowel phones in the IPA context. *Govor*, **35**, 189–214.

Vogel, I., Athanasopoulou, A. & Pincus, N. (2016). Prominence, contrast and the functional load hypothesis: An acoustic investigation. In J. Heinz, R. Goedemans and H. van der Hulst, eds., *Dimensions of Phonological Stress*. Cambridge: Cambridge University Press, pp. 123–167.

Vysotskij, S. S. (1973). O zvukovoj strukture slova v russkix govorax. In Ju. S. Azarx, S. V. Bromlej and N. Bulatova, eds., *Issledovanija po russkoj dialektologii*. Moscow: Nauka, pp. 17–41.

White, L. & Turk, A. E. (2010). English words on the procrustean bed: Polysyllabic shortening reconsidered. *Journal of Phonetics*, **38**(3), 459–471.

Wiese, R. (1996). *The Phonology of German*. Oxford: Oxford University Press.

Zales'kyj, A. M. (1973). *Vokalizm pivdenno-zaxidnyx hovoriv ukrajins'koji movy*. Kyiv: Naukova dumka.

Zaliznjak, A. A. (1985). *Od praslavjanskoj akcentuacii k russkoj*. Moscow: Nauka.

Ziłyński, J. (1932). *Opis fonetyczny języka ukraińskiego*. Krakow: Polska Akademia Umiejętności.

Žovtobrjux, M. A. (1973). *Ukrajins'ka literaturna vymova i naholos*. Kyiv: Naukova Dumka.

Acknowledgements

We would like to thank two anonymous reviewers and editor Patrycja Strycharczuk for their helpful comments and feedback. We would also like to thank the Ukrainian speakers who took part in the experiments. Last but not least, we would like to thank Anna Łukaszewicz for her support and collaboration on several papers, which were part of the Ukrainian metrical system project.

Cambridge Elements

Phonology

Robert Kennedy
University of California, Santa Barbara

Robert Kennedy is a Senior Lecturer in Linguistics at the University of California, Santa Barbara. His research has focused on segmental and rhythmic alternations in reduplicative phonology, with an emphasis on interactions among stress patterns, morphological structure, and allomorphic phenomena, and socio-phonological variation within and across the vowel systems of varieties of English. His work has appeared in *Linguistic Inquiry*, *Phonology*, and *American Speech*. He is also the author of *Phonology: A Coursebook* (Cambridge University Press), an introductory textbook for students of phonology.

Patrycja Strycharczuk
University of Manchester

Patrycja Strycharczuk is a Senior Lecturer in Linguistics and Quantitative Methods at the University of Manchester. Her research programme is centered on exploring the sound structure of language by using instrumental articulatory data. Her major research projects to date have examined the relationship between phonology and phonetics in the context of laryngeal processes, the morphology–phonetics interactions, and articulatory dynamics as a factor in sound change. The results of these investigations have appeared in journals such as *Journal of Phonetics*, *Laboratory Phonology*, and *Journal of the Acoustical Society of America*. She has received funding from the British Academy and the Arts and Humanities Research Council.

Editorial Board

Diana Archangeli, *University of Arizona*
Ricardo Bermúdez-Otero, *University of Manchester*
Jennifer Cole, *Northwestern University*
Silke Hamann, *University of Amsterdam*

About the Series

Cambridge Elements in Phonology is an innovative series that presents the growth and trajectory of phonology and its advancements in theory and methods, through an exploration of a wide range of topics, including classical problems in phonology, typological and aerial phenomena, and interfaces and extensions of phonology to neighbouring disciplines.

Cambridge Elements

Phonology

Elements in the Series

Coarticulation in Phonology
Georgia Zellou

Complexity in the Phonology of Tone
Lian-Hee Wee and Mingxing Li

Quantitative and Computational Approaches to Phonology
Jane Chandlee

Psycholinguistics and Phonology: The Forgotten Foundations of Generative Phonology
Naiyan Du and Karthik Durvasula

Issues in Metrical Phonology: Insights from Ukrainian
Beata Łukaszewicz and Janina Mołczanow

A full series listing is available at: www.cambridge.org/EPHO

www.ingramcontent.com/pod-product-compliance
Ingram Content Group UK Ltd.
Pitfield, Milton Keynes, MK11 3LW, UK
UKHW020517100325
455776UK00024BA/669

9 781009 447140